Michail Laue 3^{ccc}

The Nobel Banquets

Modern Recipes from Classic Menus

You say I am a
For all of us are
Begun in pain,
This breathing clay h

ddle — it may be

ddles une; released.

deeper torture ended,

t business has it here?

THE POEM "YOU SAY I AM A RIDDLE" WAS WRITTEN BY ALFRED NOBEL AT THE AGE OF 18.

Contents

Invite your friends
to a Nobel dinner at home.
The recipes in this book
are for six people.

The First Nobel Banquet

It is not difficult to imagine the discussion amongst the committee who organised the first Nobel Celebrations in 1901.

– This is an opportunity not to be missed. We simply must put Stockholm on the map and show the best that the city has to offer.

– In that case the Grand Hôtel is the obvious place to put up the laureates and hold the Nobel supper.

– But where will we distribute the Nobel Prizes?

– It must be a location that shows modern Sweden at its best. What do you say to the Royal Academy of Music?

– Yes, we must set a high standard from the start… Who will hand out the prizes?

– I think that we…

– Wait, I have an idea. Just think if we could get the king to do it…

– Brilliant.

And that was what happened – almost. The king, Oscar II, was unfortunately obliged to decline handing out the Nobel Prizes in 1901 because "royal duties called him to his brother country" (he was also king of Norway, at that time under Swedish rule). Crown Prince Gustav did it instead and so the Nobel event was granted royal patronage.

THE FIRST NOBEL AWARDS CEREMONY IN 1901
AT THE ROYAL SWEDISH ACADEMY OF MUSIC.

THE KITCHEN AT THE GRAND HÔTEL IN 1901.
IT WAS POSSIBLE TO COOK 1000 STEAKS AT
ONCE WITH THESE MODERN OVENS.

OTHER FEATURES INCLUDED WATER HEATERS
GRILLS AND GRIDDLES, WHERE THE DRIPPING
AND GREASE COLLECTED.

It was important that everything was perfectly arranged, and there was every chance of success. The Grand Hôtel had recently been completely renovated, making it one of Europe's most modern hotels. The interior decor was elegant and sophisticated. The wine cellar contained 120,000 bottles, three times as many as a top-class French restaurant could offer. The kitchen boasted the most up-to-date facilities; its ovens were the finest in the world. The hotel had also acquired en suite bathrooms – a great innovation at that time. The Hall of Mirrors gleamed gold and white.

It was in the Hall of Mirrors that the Nobel laureates and the invited guests were to dine after the awards ceremony.

150 guests were invited to the first ceremony of the Nobel Foundation. Only men were invited and they were all expected to wear full evening dress. However it was not easy to organise so many men in evening suits in 1901. Those in charge solved this problem by including men from the Swedish legal profession and from the government on the guest list. 150 people were, however, nowhere near enough to fill the galleries in the Royal Swedish Academy of Music. Even this problem was elegantly overcome; the gentlemen's servants were quite simply invited along to swell the numbers.

The subsequent supper was, of course, also an all-male affair. The cost of the supper was 15 Swedish kronor per head (at 1901 prices, approximately $220 in 1998). For this amount they were provided with a seven course menu and champagne, an unusual drink for the time.

Alfred's nephew, Emanuel Nobel, took part in the first awards ceremony. As the night wore on he treated the guests to Russian caviar and champagne

EMANUEL NOBEL 1859 – 1932
HE PLAYED AN IMPORTANT PART IN GETTING THE RELATIVES
TO COME TO AN AGREEMENT CONCERNING ALFRED'S WILL.

KING OSCAR II 1829 – 1907

as well as further entertainment. The festivities following the banquet became a tradition, which was later adopted by Stockholm's student union organisations.

The Nobel Festivities grows

From the very first awards ceremony in 1901 it has always been Sweden's king or, under certain circumstances, the crown prince who hands over the prizes. But every rule has its exceptions. When Oscar II fell ill and died two days before the prize giving in 1907, the celebratory ceremonies including the banquet were cancelled, and the prizes were handed out by the Nobel Foundation's chairman. The First and Second World Wars also put paid to the Nobel ceremonies, and during the war years there were neither prizes nor celebrations. During the Hungarian Uprising of 1956, the banquet was replaced by a simpler meal at the Swedish Academy.

The Nobel Prizes and festivities grew in popularity. In 1926, the awards ceremony was moved to the newly built Concert Hall to make room for more guests. A few years later, the evening banquet moved to the City Hall, as the Grand Hôtel's Hall of Mirrors could not accommodate all the guests. The Grand Hôtel is, however, still the hotel where the laureates and their families stay.

Until 1909 the names of the laureates were kept secret until the 10th December. But over the years, the advance announcement of the laureates' names has become almost as important as the ceremonies on the day. Interest in the Nobel Prizes is enormous and in today's media-driven society

THE GRAND HÔTEL'S HALL
OF MIRRORS IN 1931.

the winners and the royal family appear in all their splendour in the superbly arranged Nobel celebrations.

Women take part

After the all-male banquet of 1901, it was decided that women should be invited. So at the next year's banquet there were women present. And in the following year, 1903, the first female laureate, Marie Curie, was handed the Nobel Prize for Physics along with her husband, Pierre Curie, by Oscar II

"in recognition of the extraordinary services they have rendered by their joint researches on the radiation phenomena discovered by Professor Henri Becquerel".

The first woman to hand over the Nobel Prizes will be Sweden's Crown Princess Victoria.

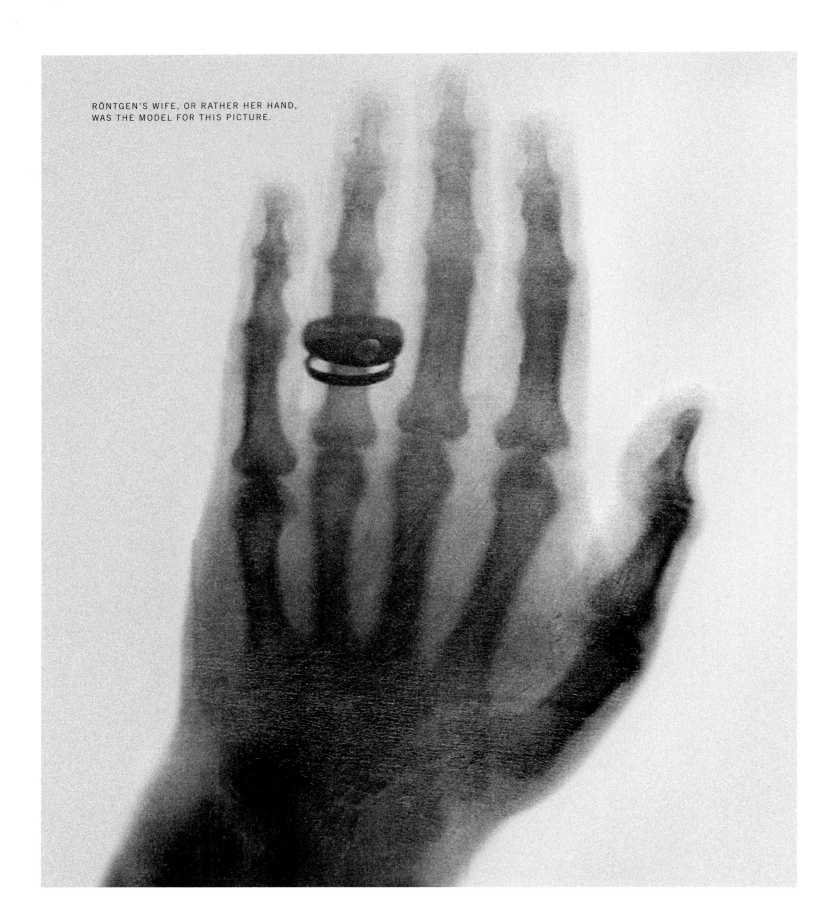

RÖNTGEN'S WIFE, OR RATHER HER HAND,
WAS THE MODEL FOR THIS PICTURE.

1901

During the first year of the Nobel Prizes the *Belle Époque* was still prevalent in Europe. At the Vollard Gallery in Paris the young Picasso had his first exhibition. It was not a public success.

In Stockholm the Royal Swedish Academy of Sciences awarded the Nobel Prize for Physics to the German, *Wilhelm Röntgen*. It was a choice which would have been approved by Nobel himself – X-rays have revolutionised medical diagnostics and opened the door to new discoveries in the field of physics. The Nobel Prize for Chemistry went to the Dutchman, *Jacobus van't Hoff*, who laid the foundations of stereochemistry and broke new ground with his brilliant hypotheses on physical chemistry.

The Karolinska Institute awarded a German researcher, *Emil von Behring*, the Nobel Prize for Medicine. His serum therapy against tetanus and diphtheria is one of the many victories over fatal diseases, which we take for granted today.

The Swedish Academy gave the Nobel Prize for Literature to the idealistic French poet, *René Sully-Prudhomme*, but was sharply criticised for passing over Leo Tolstoy.

In Oslo the Nobel Peace Prize was divided between the Swiss founder of the Red Cross, *Henri Dunant*, and the French campaigner for peace, *Frédéric Passy*.

1901

GOLDEN GOBLETS AND CUT CRYSTAL. BEAUTIFULLY FOLDED NAPKINS AND SMALL BISCUITS FOR DECORATION. A FITTING AND MAGNIFICENT SETTING FOR A CLASSIC DINNER.

First Course 1901

Hors d'œuvres – Tasty Appetisers

Hors d'œuvres is French and means "outside the work". Today the expression refers to the cold or hot appetisers or snacks which precede a meal. Previously such appetisers could be served at any time during the meal. In 1901 these hors d'œuvres were probably served as appetisers to judge by the extent of the menu.

We are offering six different appetisers. Most can be prepared well in advance of the dinner itself. Two or three per person would make a reasonable first course. If you only choose one of them, the recipe should be doubled or tripled to feed six people.

Wild mushroom salad (picture)
Slice 300 g (10 oz) small wild mushrooms (Boletus edulis or cep mushrooms were used here). Fry them in 2 tbsp olive oil. Add salt and pepper. Blend 50 ml (3 1/2 tbsp) olive oil, 2 tbsp balsamic vinegar and a crushed garlic clove to make the dressing. Halve, remove pulp and then chop 3 tomatoes. Finely chop 1 red onion. Mix the tomatoes and onions with the dressing. Place in a bowl and crown the salad with the mushrooms and chopped parsley.

Nizza beans
Wash 250 g (1/2 lb) fresh green beans. Boil for 1 minute in lightly salted water. Drain and cool immediately by pouring cold water over them. Allow 1 x 400 g (14 oz) tin of tomatoes to drain through a sieve. Fry 1 finely chopped onion and 1 finely chopped clove of garlic in oil. Flavour with 1 tbsp tarragon and a pinch of black pepper. Add the chopped tomatoes. Simmer for about 5 minutes. Add 2 tbsp capers. Put the beans into small bundles. Spoon over the tomato mixture, and decorate with olives, for example, black anchovy-stuffed olives.

Salmon salad
Layer 3 sliced tomatoes with 3 pre-cooked sliced almond potatoes and 75 g (2 1/2 oz) thinly sliced smoked salmon. Whisk together 100 ml (7 tbsp) oil, 2 tbsp red wine vinegar, 1 tbsp mustard and 1 tsp sugar to make the dressing. Pour it over. Sprinkle 1 tbsp finely chopped chives and 1 tbsp finely chopped red onion over the top.

Öregrund fish appetisers
Cut the fins off 6 double fillets of Baltic herring (stuffed with dill or parsley). Add salt and pepper. Lay 6 thin slices of cold smoked salmon over the fillets. Fold them in half like a wallet. Dip in breadcrumbs. Fry in butter until golden brown. Allow to cool. Serve with soured cream, a spoonful of whitefish roe and a sprig of dill.

Marinated mussels and prawns
Mix 3 tbsp oil with 100 ml (7 tbsp) white wine vinegar. Whisk in 1 tsp sugar, 1 tsp salt, a pinch of black pepper and a crushed clove of garlic. Add 1 finely chopped red onion and either 1 ordinary or 1 soured chopped pickled gherkin (about 50 ml, 3 1/2 tbsp). Then add 80 g (3 oz) peeled prawns and around 80 g (3 oz) previously shelled mussels (you will need about 1 kg (2 1/2 lb) of mussels cooked in their shells). Leave to marinate for half an hour. Add 2 tbsp chopped parsley to serve. This can be spooned onto small slices of bread which have been fried in butter.

Eggs Provençal
Hard boil 3 eggs. Shell and halve the eggs. Remove the yolks and mash them with 6 anchovy fillets. Stir in 2 tbsp mayonnaise and 1 tsp finely chopped dill. Pipe this into the egg white halves. Garnish each egg half with an anchovy.

Main Course 1901

Roast Fillet of Beef Imperial

Serves 6

1 kg (2 1/4 lb) lean fillet of beef, trimmed
salt, pepper
butter for frying
6 slices of pâté de foie gras,
about 20 g (3/4 oz) each,
or other good quality pâté
6 slices of truffle

Vegetable matchsticks:
24 small green asparagus spears,
or 12 large ones
2 carrots, about 180 g (6 oz)
3 parsnips, about 150 g (5 oz)
1 tsp sugar + 2 tsp salt + 1–2 tbsp
butter per litre of boiling water

Port and cream sauce:
150 ml (2/3 cup) port wine
50 ml (3 1/2 tbsp) veal stock (bottled)
1/2 tbsp balsamic vinegar
a pinch of black pepper
1 bay leaf
1/2 tbsp cornflour or
thickening agent (e.g. Maizena)
100 ml (1/2 cup) water
150 ml (2/3 cup) crème fraîche

Method:

Begin with the sauce. Bring the port wine and veal stock to the boil, adding the vinegar, pepper and bay leaf. Remove from the heat and allow to stand for at least 10 minutes to extract the flavour of the herbs. Set the oven at 110°C (230°F).

Add salt and pepper to the meat. Brown the beef all over by frying it in butter. Put it in the oven. Roast until the inner temperature is about 59°C (138°F, preferably measure this using a meat thermometer). Wrap the meat in greaseproof paper and let it rest for at least 10 minutes before cutting into slices.

Wash the asparagus and cut into 5 cm (2 inches) long pieces; larger asparagus should also be cut lengthways. Peel and cut the carrots and parsnips into matchsticks. Briefly boil the root vegetables in water with sugar, salt and butter until they are just soft, but still al dente. Then boil the asparagus in the same water. Drain the vegetables and keep warm.

Strain the sauce. Thicken with cornflour or equivalent thickening agent dissolved in water. Boil for 5 minutes. Put about 75 ml (5 tbsp) aside to serve. Whisk the crème fraîche into the remaining sauce so that it becomes light and airy. Taste.

Cut the meat into 6 slices. Place a circle of light sauce on each plate. Put the meat on top. Put a circle of dark sauce around the light sauce. Lay the vegetable sticks around the meat and crown the dish with pâté de foie gras and a truffle slice. A suitable accompaniment to this would be potato swirls, which can be prepared in advance. See the recipe on page 80.

Apricot Tartlet with Ice Cream

Serves 6

2 sheets of puff pastry
6 fresh apricots,
or 12 preserved apricot halves
100 ml (1/2 cup) redcurrant
or rowanberry jelly
600 ml (2 2/3 cups) vanilla ice cream

Filling:
150 g (5 oz) marzipan
75 g (2 1/2 oz) butter
2 eggs
1 tsp plain flour
1 tsp sugar
50 ml (3 1/2 tbsp) whipping cream

Apricot sauce:
5 fresh apricots,
or 10 preserved apricot halves
2 tbsp freshly squeezed lemon juice
2 tbsp sugar

Method:

Defrost the sheets of puff pastry and roll them out to double their size. Set oven at 175°C (350°F). Make the filling. Whisk the sugar and butter until it is pale and full of air. Grate the marzipan. Add the egg, flour, marzipan and cream.

Divide the puff pastry into 6 pieces. Line 6 individual baking tins with the pastry. Cut away excess pastry. Fill the tins until 3/4 full with the marzipan mixture. Bake the tartlets in the centre of the oven for about 15 minutes. Allow to cool.

For the sauce, blend the stoned apricots with the lemon juice and sugar until they form a fine purée. Dilute with a little apricot juice or water if necessary.

Slice the remaining apricots. Heat the jelly. Arrange the apricot slices over the tartlets and pour over the jelly.

Serve the tartlets on a circle of sauce with a scoop of vanilla ice cream.

Tip: An easier way of making the apricot sauce is to use 1 tin of apricot purée baby food and add lemon juice and sugar to taste.

1913

For fifteen years, rapid economic growth had tripled the production of iron, coal and oil in the industrialised world and the standard of living had increased for large numbers of people. But the clouds of war were looming; six months after the Nobel Prize ceremony the First World War broke out.

The Nobel Prize for Physics went to the Dutchman, *Heike Kamerlingh Onnes,* for his pioneering contribution to low temperature physics. *Alfred Werner,* who was Swiss, received the Nobel Prize for Chemistry for his work on molecular compounds and the bonding of atoms in inorganic molecules.

The Nobel Prize for Physiology or Medicine was awarded to the Frenchman, *Charles Richet,* for his identification of the immune system response known as anaphylactic shock – a life-threatening allergic reaction against foreign proteins and antigens.

The Indian poet and playwright, *Rabindranath Tagore,* was the first non-European to win the Nobel Prize for Literature. He wrote in both Bengali and English and is seen as something of a bridge builder between the east and the west.

The Nobel Committee in Oslo gave the Peace Prize to the Belgian politician, *Henri La Fontaine,* a prominent figure in the European peace movement.

THE INAUGURATION OF THE LARGEST RAILWAY STATION IN
THE WORLD, GRAND CENTRAL STATION IN NEW YORK.

1913 RUSTIC SIMPLICITY MEETS
LUXURY AND FINESSE.

First Course 1913

Luxury Turbot Entrée

Serves 6

6 turbot fillets weighing
about 100 g (3 1/2 oz)
1 tbsp butter
2 tbsp finely chopped shallots
salt, white pepper
100 ml (1/2 cup) white wine
100 ml (1/2 cup) water or fish stock
6 lobster claws
6 thin slices of truffle
6 mushroom tops

White wine sauce:
1/2 onion
2 tbsp butter
1 1/2 tbsp flour
50 ml (3 1/2 tbsp) fish essence (bottled)
150 ml (2/3 cup) white wine
300 ml (1 1/3 cups) whipping cream
salt, white pepper

Method:

Begin with the sauce. Finely chop the onion. Fry it in butter but without browning. Sprinkle over the flour and stir. Add the fish essence, wine and cream. Allow to cook for several minutes. Add salt and white pepper to taste. Keep warm. Set oven at 125°C (260°F).

Grease an ovenproof dish. Spread the chopped onion in the bottom. Lay the fish fillets on top. Add salt and pepper. Pour over the wine and water/stock so that it covers the fish. Cover with a lid or greaseproof paper. Cook in the oven for about 15 minutes until the fish meat is white.

Heat the lobster claws, truffle slices and mushroom tops in the stock used to cook the fish.

Arrange the fish fillets on warmed plates. Pour over the sauce. Garnish with lobster claws, truffle slices and mushroom tops. For extra taste in this dish stir a little lobster essence (bottled) into the white wine sauce.

Tip: If lobster claws and truffles are difficult to obtain, substitute with, for example, crayfish tails and salmon roe.

Main Course 1913

Chicken Breast with Early Spring Vegetables

Serves 6

3 chickens
salt, white pepper
butter for frying

Early Spring Vegetables:
18 silverskin onions
250 g (1/2 lb) green beans
2 red onions
1 tsp olive oil
salt, white pepper

Beef marrow sauce:
300 ml (1 1/3 cups) red wine
4 tbsp concentrated
beef stock (bottled)
2 tbsp brown sugar
2 bay leaves
a pinch of white pepper
1 onion
1 tbsp butter
1 tsp cornflour or equivalent
thickening agent such as
Maizena + 1 tbsp white wine
150 g (5 oz) sliced beef marrow
(order slices of beef marrow
bone several days in advance)

Method:

Begin with the sauce. Bring the wine, concentrated beef stock, sugar, bay leaves and white pepper to the boil and cook for several minutes. Remove from the heat and leave to stand for at least 10 minutes so that the sauce can extract the flavour from the herbs.

Now for the vegetables. Peel and cook the silverskin onions in lightly salted water. Top and tail the green beans and cut in half. Peel the red onion and cut into segments. Bring the vegetables quickly to the boil, then cool rapidly in ice cold water.

Set the oven to 110°C (230°F). Cut off the drumsticks. Trim the area under the legs. Cut off the breast fillets so that they are separated from the legs. Brown the chicken pieces all over in the butter. Add salt and pepper. Then roast in the oven for a further twenty minutes so that the inner temperature reaches at least 73°C (164°F) (preferably measure this by using a meat thermometer). The breast meat will be ready before the leg meat. Remove and allow the chicken pieces to rest for 5–10 minutes before slicing.

Peel and finely chop the onion for the sauce. Fry it in butter but without browning. Pour over the sauce. Bring to the boil and thicken with cornflour or Maizena dissolved in wine. Dilute the sauce with a little water if it seems too thick/strong. Heat the marrow slices in the sauce.

Heat the vegetables in a little olive oil and water. Flavour with salt and white pepper. Pile up the vegetables. Arrange a few breast slices among them. Place the drumsticks on top and pour over the sauce. Accompany with Massenet Potatoes. See the recipe on page 85.

Dessert 1913

Vanilla Ice Cream Rolled in Nougat with Chocolate Sauce

Serves 6

600 ml (2 2/3 cups) vanilla ice cream

Nougat:
200 g (7 oz) peeled almonds
350 ml (1 1/2 cups) sugar
3 tbsp glucose
(available from chemists)
cooking oil

Chocolate Sauce:
200 ml (1 cup) stout
100 ml (7 tbsp) sugar
4–5 tbsp cocoa powder
1 tsp vanilla powder
2 tbsp blackcurrant jelly
1–2 tbsp lemon juice

Method:

Begin with the nougat. Set the oven at 175°C (350°F). Lay the almonds onto a baking tray. Roast them in the centre of the oven until golden brown.

Mix the sugar and glucose in a thick-based saucepan. Heat and keep stirring so that the sugar caramelises without turning dark in colour. Add the roasted almonds and mix together. Pour into a well-oiled tray with sides. Allow to cool. Break into lumps.

For the chocolate sauce, blend all of the ingredients in a large pan. Heat gently until the sauce comes to the boil, then remove from the heat and allow to cool. Whisk before serving.

Divide the ice cream into 6 blocks. Roll the edges in the crushed nougat. Place the ice cream onto plates and encircle with chocolate sauce.

Tip: A strawberry and/or a small chocolate petit fours or chocolate dipped biscuit enhances this dessert.

Alfred Nobel

When the Nobel Prizes are distributed on the 10th December, millions of people all over the world follow the impressive ceremony in the Concert Hall in Stockholm. One by one, the annual prize winners receive their medals and certificates from the hands of the king of Sweden. In the background sits a bronze statue of Alfred Nobel himself, looking down on the celebrations.

It may even be possible to imagine a faint smile under the full beard. Nobel was no supporter of royalty, but he was quite familiar with their popular appeal. In this, as in so much else, he was full of contradictions: an optimist about the future and a misanthrope, a peace-lover and an arms manufacturer, an idealistic benefactor and a tough businessman, spiritual and outgoing and yet introspective too.

> *"You say I am a riddle – it may be*
> *For all of us are riddles unexplained.*
> *Begun in pain, in deeper torture ended,*
> *This breathing clay, what business has it here?"*
>
> ALFRED NOBEL

In 1851, during his stay in Paris, Alfred Nobel sat and wrote a long autobiographical poem. In the poem *"You say I am a Riddle"* he describes his tragic love for a young girl who died of consumption. Alfred was only 18 years old and found himself at a crossroads in his life. His poem was a farewell

ALFRED NOBEL 1833 – 1896

ALFRED NOBEL AT THE AGE OF 50. THIS IS ONE OF
THE FEW EXISTING PHOTOGRAPHS OF THE FOUNDER
OF THE NOBEL PRIZES.

IMMANUEL NOBEL 1801 – 1872

ALFRED INHERITED TENACITY AND A WEALTH
OF DISCOVERIES FROM HIS FATHER WHO WAS AN
ARCHITECT, MASTER BUILDER, ENGINEER AND
INDEFATIGABLE INNOVATOR, AND REMAINED OPTI-
MISTIC DESPITE MISFORTUNE AND BANKRUPTCY.

ANDRIETTA NOBEL 1803 – 1889

ALFRED'S MOTHER WAS THE MOST IMPORTANT WOMAN
IN HIS LIFE AND SHE REMAINED ALFRED'S STAUNCHEST
SUPPORTER RIGHT UP TO HER DEATH. DURING THE DIFFI-
CULT YEARS OF POVERTY IN STOCKHOLM AT THE END OF
THE 1830S WHEN IMMANUEL WAS TRYING TO ESTABLISH
A NEW FUTURE IN ST. PETERSBURG, IT WAS ANDRIETTA
WHO HELD TOGETHER AND CARED FOR THE FAMILY.

to love; he would now devote himself to science.

The poem was also a farewell to his dreams of becoming a writer. Alfred's father Immanuel had made it clear to his son that after several years abroad, he was to involve himself in the family's engineering business in St. Petersburg.

Alfred was already a man of the world. He spoke Swedish, Russian, English, French, German and later Italian. He had received a first class private education and was now studying chemistry in Paris. There he became acquainted with a subject which was to remain his passion throughout his life: nitroglycerine.

"We cannot expect an effective explosive
to become commonly used without the loss of life."
ALFRED NOBEL

In 1846 the Italian chemist Ascanio Sobrero experimented with nitration and dripped glycerine into a mixture of sulphur and nitric acid. The test tube exploded in his face. This was how nitroglycerine first demonstrated its unpredictable explosive quality. He warned colleagues to beware of the dangerous liquid.

But at the beginning of the 1860s Alfred Nobel was determined to make industrial use of this material discovered by science. Nitroglycerine was ten times stronger than gunpowder and fairly simple to produce; the problem lay in controlling the explosion.

Nobel's brainwave was to use a small wooden casing, filled with gunpowder and equipped with a fuse. The charge of gunpowder sent a shock wave through the nitroglycerine and caused it to detonate. With his innovative fuse, Alfred Nobel paved the way for the first new explosive since gunpowder had been introduced in the 15th century. Of all his 355 different patents, this was perhaps the most important.

In the summer of 1864 Alfred and his father began to manufacture explosive oil on a small scale near the family home at Heleneborg in Stockholm. The laboratory exploded on 3rd September and five people died, including Alfred's younger brother Emil. The first human lives had been sacrificed; many more were to follow.

Despite the accident, Nobel received a large order for the explosive oil to be used during the construction of the south tunnel under Stockholm. In the same year he founded the Nitroglycerine Company, but his plans were more far reaching than that.

"I live where I work and I work in all countries."
ALFRED NOBEL

Nobel had many talents, both as an inventor and a businessman. He lived in the golden age of industrialisation and his explosive oil became a success during the frantic expansion of mines and railways. But in 1866, when the production of explosive oil had just begun at Nobel's factory in Germany, a series of catastrophic accidents took place in Europe, Australia and America. Hundreds of people lost their lives when nitroglycerine exploded without warning. Nobel was forced to radically improve his explosive.

Three years earlier he had had the idea of mixing nitroglycerine with

ALFRED NOBEL WAS PARTICULAR ABOUT SAFETY BUT MANY SERIOUS ACCIDENTS OCCURRED AT HIS DYNAMITE FACTORIES. TWELVE PEOPLE DIED WHEN THE FACTORY AT VINTERVIKEN WAS ALMOST COMPLETELY DESTROYED IN A SERIES OF EXPLOSIONS IN 1874.

THE FIRST VERSION OF THE INNOVATIVE FUSE CONSISTED SIMPLY OF A CORKED WOODEN
CASING FILLED WITH GUNPOWDER, WHICH WAS SUBMERGED IN NITROGLYCERINE.

IN THE MIDDLE OF THE 1860S THE GUNPOWDER WAS REPLACED WITH FULMINATING MERCURY,
CONTAINED IN A COPPER CAP.

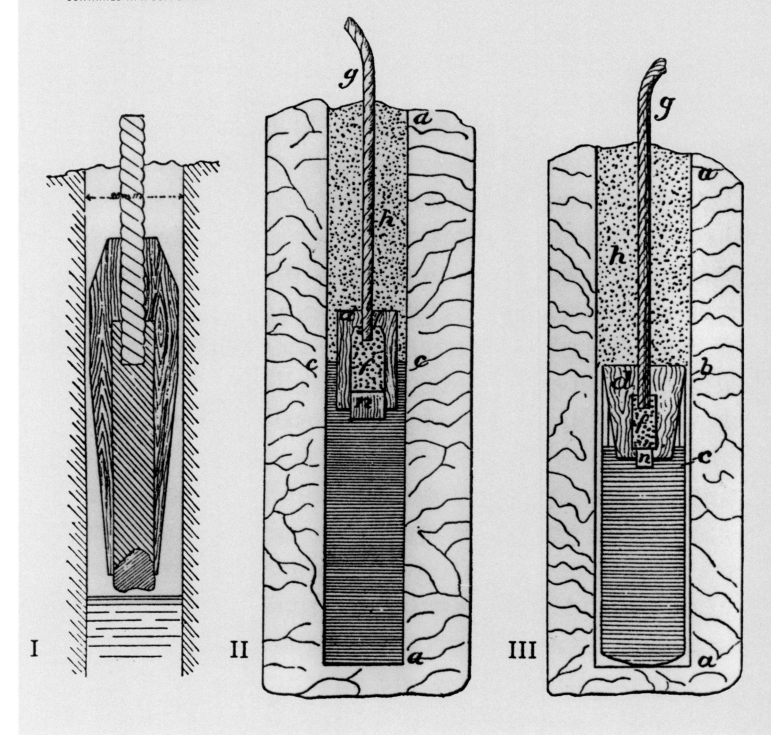

PATENT-URKUNDE

№ 36872

AUF GRUND DER ANGEHEFTETEN BESCHREIBUNG IST DURCH BESCHLUSS
DES KAISERLICHEN PATENTAMTES

Alfred Nobel in Paris

EIN PATENT ERTHEILT WORDEN.

GEGENSTAND DES PATENTES IST:

Gefahrlose Explosivstoffe.

GESETZ v. 25. MAI 1877

ANFANG DES PATENTES: *4. August 1885.*

DIE RECHTE UND PFLICHTEN DES PATENT-INHABERS SIND DURCH DAS PATENT-GESETZ
VOM 25. MAI 1877 (REICHSGESETZBLATT FÜR 1877 SEITE 501) BESTIMMT.

ZU URKUND DER ERTHEILUNG DES PATENTES IST DIESE AUSFERTIGUNG
ERFOLGT.

Berlin, *den 28 September 1886.*

KAISERLICHES PATENTAMT.

Beglaubigt durch *Guthke.*

Sekretär des Kaiserlichen Patentamtes.

Wegen der Patentgebühren ist die zweite und letzte Seite dieser Urkunde zu beachten!

4 aug. 1885

F. 2.

powdered charcoal to form a plastic substance, which could be used in horizontal bore holes. After many experiments with different absorbent materials, Alfred discovered that a silicon packing material, kieselguhr (also known as diatomite), the sand which surrounded his German factory, could absorb three times its own weight in nitroglycerine. The mixture, a reddish yellow putty-like paste, completely neutralised nitroglycerine's volatile properties.

Alfred called his invention *dynamite* and had it patented in the UK in 1867. Travelling extensively around Europe, he demonstrated its safety by throwing boxes of dynamite down a hill then setting fire to them. He always carried with him a case containing three sticks of dynamite in his inside pocket and would frighten dinner guests by hitting the sticks against the edge of the table as hard as he could and then putting them in his mouth and setting fire to them.

Ten years and innumerable setbacks later, Alfred Nobel had set up dynamite companies in twelve countries. He was then one of Europe's richest men, a multinational one-man band without even a personal secretary. He settled in Paris and worked harder than ever. In 1875 he discovered an even safer and more effective explosive - gelatinised nitrocellulose created via the unlikely combination of two highly explosive materials, nitrocellulose and nitroglycerine.

Nobel's focus changed during the 1880s military rearmament and he discovered ballistite, an ingenious smokeless powder which was also based on nitrocellulose and nitroglycerine. At the beginning of the 1890s he bought the Bofors works and laid the foundations for an international Swedish arms industry.

> *"The capital, invested in safe securities by my executors, shall constitute a fund, the interest on which shall be annually distributed in the form of prizes to those who, during the preceding year, shall have conferred the greatest benefit on mankind."*
> FROM ALFRED NOBEL'S WILL

In November 1895, worn out and suffering from heart disease, Nobel sat and wrote his will in Paris. It shows his faith in the future of science and his interest in literature and peace but also his distrust of mankind's motives and of inherited wealth. His relatives received only minor sums of money as bequests; this led to trouble.

Alfred Nobel died of a cerebral haemorrhage on December 10th, 1896 at the age of 63, alone in his villa in San Remo. The terms of his will were greeted with wonder by many but dismissed by others. In the beginning even the Swedish king, Oscar II, stated that Nobel *"has been influenced by peace fanatics, especially women"*. The king was referring to Nobel's friend Bertha von Suttner, who was one of the most prominent figures in the European peace movement.

Nationalists were incensed by the will's wording that "the most worthy shall receive the prize, whether he be Scandinavian or not". The proposed prize awarding institutions hesitated and Nobel's Swedish relatives took the matter to court to have the will declared invalid.

Testament

Jag undertecknad Alfred Bernhard Nobel förklarar härmed efter moget betänkande min yttersta vilja i afseende å den egendom jag vid min död kan efterlemna vara följande:

Öfver hela min återstående realiserbara förmögenhet förfogas på följande sätt: Kapitalet, af utredningsmännen realiseradt till säkra värdepapper, skall utgöra en fond hvars ränta årligen utdelas som prisbelöning åt dem som under det förlupne året hafva gjort menskligheten den största nytta. Räntan delas i fem lika delar som tillfalla: en del den som inom fysikens område har gjort den vigtigaste upptäckt eller uppfinning; en del den som har gjort den vigtigaste kemiska upptäckt eller förbättring; en del den som har gjort den vigtigaste upptäckt inom fysiologiens eller medicinens område; en del den som inom literaturen har producerat det utmärktaste i idealisk rigtning; och en del åt den som har verkat mest eller best för folkens förbrödrande och afskaffande eller minskning af stående armeer samt bildande och spridande af fredskongresser. Priset för fysik och kemi utdelas af Svenska Vetenskapsakademien; för fysiologiska eller medicinska arbeten af Carolinska Institutet i Stockholm; för literatur af Akademien i Stockholm samt för fredsförfäktare af ett utskott af fem personer som väljas af Norska Stortinget. Det är min uttryckliga vilja att vid prisutdelningarne intet afseende fästes vid någon slags nationalitetstillhörighet sålunda att den värdigaste erhåller priset antingen han är Skandinav eller ej.

Detta testamente är ännu rätteligen det enda giltiga och upphäfver alla mina föregående testamentariska bestämmelser om sådane skulle förefinnas efter min död.

Slutligen anordnar jag dödom varande min uttryckliga önskan och vilja att efter min död pulsådrorne uppskäras och att sedan detta skett och tydliga dödstecken af kompetente läkare intygats liket förbrännas i såkallad crematorieugn.

Paris den 27 November
1895
Alfred Bernhard Nobel

RAGNAR SOHLMAN 1870 – 1948

RAGNAR SOHLMAN WAS EMPLOYED
BY ALFRED NOBEL IN 1893 AND
SOON BECAME A COLLEAGUE AND
CLOSE FRIEND.

Chemist Ragnar Sohlman was only 26 when he found out that his deceased employer and friend Alfred Nobel had made him an executor of his will, along with the engineer Rudolf Lilljeqvist. Sohlman was immediately put under enormous pressure to be reasonable and to refrain from carrying out Nobel's "fantastic idea". However he did not do so. Mostly thanks to Sohlman's diplomacy, persistence and unconventional methods, a settlement was finally reached with the relatives after more than a year of bitter wrangling.

In June 1900 the Nobel Foundation was finally established and the following year the first prizes were given out. Crown Prince Gustav officiated at the ceremony in Stockholm, but in 1902 Oscar II began the tradition of the head of state giving out the prizes. Alfred Nobel could not have wished for better publicity for his vision.

ALBERT EINSTEIN WHO WAS AWARDED
THE 1921 PHYSICS PRIZE "FOR HIS
SERVICES TO THEORETICAL PHYSICS,
AND ESPECIALLY FOR HIS DISCOVERY
OF THE LAW OF THE PHOTOELECTRIC
EFFECT."

1926

Classical physics was shaken to the core, first by Einstein's Theory of Relativity and then by quantum mechanics. Television, the first apparatus for transmitting moving pictures, was invented. For the first time ordinary people could hear the Nobel Prize awards ceremony via live radio broadcast.

The French physicist, *Jean Perrin*, was honoured with the Nobel Prize for Physics for his studies of Brownian motion and sedimentation equilibrium (the fact that microscopic particles in a liquid do not sink to the bottom due to molecular movement), which proved the existence of atoms and molecules. The Nobel Prize for Chemistry went to Sweden's *"The" Svedberg* for his work with colloids.

Johannes Fibiger, from Denmark, received the Nobel Prize for Medicine for inducing intestinal cancer in rats and thereby stimulating cancer research, which was still in its infancy.

The Nobel Prize for Literature was given to the Italian author, *Grazia Deledda*, who based the plots for her many novels on her childhood in a remote Sardinian village.

The French foreign minister, *Aristide Briand*, and his German colleague, *Gustav Stresemann*, were awarded the Nobel Peace Prize. They had opened the channels of communication between the two former enemies and worked to achieve the Treaty of Locarno the previous year.

1926

WARMTH AND WILD GAME TOGETHER.
HUNTING AND FIRE. SIMPLE TRADITION.

Game Consommé with Croutons

Serves 6

4 egg whites
300 g (10 oz) finely chopped vegetables
(carrot, celery and onion)
300 g (10 oz) minced game
matchsticks from 1 x 6 cm
(1/2 x 2 1/2 inches) long carrot
100 g (3 1/2 oz) preserved wild
mushrooms (morels used here)
butter for frying

Game Stock:
2 litres (9 cups) water
100 ml (7 tbsp) sherry
600 ml (2 2/3 cups) red wine
300 ml (1 1/3 cups) concentrated
game stock (bottled)
2 tbsp crushed juniper berries
1 tsp ground white pepper

Croutons:
6 slices of white bread without crusts
olive oil for frying
game spice

Method:

Begin with the game stock. Bring the various ingredients to the boil, then allow to stand and extract the flavour for at least ten minutes. Pour through a sieve and let the liquid cool.

Whisk the egg whites until they form a light foam. Mix with the vegetables and game mince. Put into a large pan. Pour on the cold stock. Heat very slowly, stirring carefully, especially at the bottom of the pan. Bring to simmering point but do not allow to boil. Then simmer carefully for 30 minutes.

Lift out the solidified egg whites, which will have floated to the edges. Sieve the stock through muslin or any other fine filter. Reheat the consommé just before serving and taste.

Parboil the carrot matchsticks and fry the mushrooms in butter. Cut the slices of bread into cubes. Fry in olive oil until golden brown. Add game spice or herbs to taste. Serve the consommé in heated soup bowls. Place the carrots and mushrooms into the soup and serve the croutons alongside. Guests should add these bit by bit so that they do not go soggy.

An authentic game consommé should have a strong game flavour as well as being completely clear and unclouded by particles. This is achieved by starting with a good concentrated game stock (or beef extract, if game stock is unavailable). The ordinary stock is made with whisked egg whites and minced game.

Marinated Fillet of Lamb with Mustard Sauce and Vegetables

Serves 6

6 x 150 g (5 oz) lamb fillets
oil for frying

Marinade:
2 cloves of garlic
2 tsp thyme
2 tsp rosemary
100 ml (1/2 cup) olive oil

Mustard Sauce:
300 ml (1 1/3 cups) red wine
4 tbsp concentrated
veal stock (bottled)
2 tbsp brown sugar
1 tsp thyme
1 tsp rosemary
1 clove of garlic
3 tbsp finely chopped onion
2 tbsp finely cubed carrot
butter for frying
1 tbsp yellow mustard seeds
1 tbsp cornflour or thickening
agent (Maizena) + 1 tbsp wine
salt, pepper

Accompaniment:
3 bulbs of fennel or
6 baby fennel bulbs
3 beetroots
melted butter
salt, pepper

Method:

Begin with the marinade. Peel and crush the cloves of garlic. Mix with the thyme, rosemary and olive oil. Place lamb fillets in a plastic bag. Pour in the marinade and make sure it covers the meat. Refrigerate and leave for at least 24 hours.

To make the sauce pour the wine and concentrated stock into a pan. Stir in the sugar, thyme and rosemary. Cook for several minutes, then allow to stand and extract the flavour from the herbs for 10–15 minutes. Peel and crush the garlic. Fry the garlic, onion and carrots in a little butter together with the mustard seeds. Pour the sauce over and cook for 1–2 minutes. Stir the thickening agent and wine together. Add slowly whilst stirring constantly. Bring to the boil and allow to simmer for a few minutes. Add salt and pepper to taste. Keep warm. Dilute the sauce with a little water if it is too thick/strong.

Set the oven at 110°C (230°F). Remove lamb fillets from the marinade and remove the herbs. Brown the fillets all over in oil. Cook for a few minutes longer in the oven until the meat is pink inside 65°C (150°F). Add salt and pepper. Roll the fillets in greaseproof paper and keep warm.

Cook the fennel bulbs and the beetroot separately in lightly salted water. Peel the beetroots. Cut them and the fennel bulbs into segments and brush with melted butter. Add salt and pepper.

Cut the lamb fillets into thin slices. Arrange on warmed plates with the vegetables, sauce and an accompaniment such as creamed potato bake. See the recipe on page 83.

Dessert 1926

Fruit Marinated in Maraschino with Ice Cream

Serves 6

1 large or 2 small pineapples
3 bananas
500 g (1 lb) strawberries

Maraschino marinade:
4 tbsp Maraschino (cherry liqueur)
200 ml (1 cup) sugar solution
(150 ml (2/3 cup) sugar +
150 ml (2/3 cup) water)
3 tbsp freshly squeezed lime juice

Accompaniment:
6 scoops of vanilla ice cream

Method:

Peel/wash fruit. Cut into small pieces.

Mix the marinade ingredients together. Pour over the fruit. Refrigerate and allow to extract the flavour for at least half an hour.

Serve the fruit with the marinade and a scoop of vanilla ice cream – remember to remove the ice cream from the freezer about half an hour before it is to be served so that it is not too hard.

Tip: Vary the fruit according to taste or season.

GRETA GARBO MADE HER SCREEN
BREAKTHROUGH IN TALKIES.

1931

The Great Depression, caused by the Wall Street Crash of 1929, cast its shadow over the world with financial crises, galloping inflation and mass unemployment. In Sweden, there was also a major shock in 1932, when the international match manufacturing business owned by Ivar Kreuger collapsed, and he committed suicide in Paris. Elsewhere in Paris, the Abstract-Creation School of Art was formed and staged joint exhibitions. One of its most famous members was Piet Mondrian.

No Nobel Prize for Physics was handed out this year. The Nobel Prize for Chemistry went to the German chemists, *Carl Bosch* and *Friedrich Bergius,* who discovered advanced high pressure methods for the chemical industry.

Even the Nobel Prize for Medicine went to a German, the aristocratic biochemist, *Otto Warburg.* He received the prize for his experiments with the enzyme which controls the oxidation process in the cells' "engine-room", mitochondrion.

The popular countryside poet, *Erik Axel Karlfeldt,* became the third Swede to receive the Nobel Prize for Literature after Selma Lagerlöf and Verner von Heidenstam. He was awarded this posthumously and the Academy was strongly criticised for the decision.

The Nobel Peace Prize was shared by two Americans – the legendary social pioneer and peace campaigner, *Jane Addams,* and Columbia University's colourful and authoritarian vice chancellor, *Nicholas Murray Butler.*

1931

BLUE SKY MEETS BLUE SEA. A LIGHT SALTY
BREEZE AND A TASTE OF SPRING.

First Course 1931

Cream of Mushroom Soup

Serves 6

600 g (1 lb 5 oz) fresh mushrooms
butter for frying
500 ml (2 1/4 cups) whipping cream
100 ml (7 tbsp) port wine
4 tbsp chicken stock
concentrate (bottled)
200 ml (1 cup) milk
white pepper, a little salt
200 ml (1 cup) crème fraîche

Accompaniment:
100 ml (1/2 cup) crème fraîche
60 g (2 oz) salmon roe

Method:

Cut the mushrooms into 3–4 mm (1/8 inch) thick slices. Fry them carefully in butter in a large, thick-bottomed pan.

Pour over the cream, port wine and chicken concentrate. Cook for about 10 minutes, stirring occasionally.

Stir in the milk. Bring to the boil and season with white pepper and a little salt. Keep warm until it is served. Whisk in the crème fraîche just before serving so that the soup is frothy.

Serve in warm soup bowls. Garnish with a spoonful of whipped crème fraîche and salmon roe.

Main Course 1931

Rolled Fillets of Sole with Shellfish Sauce and Leeks

Serves 6

12 fillets of sole (3 sole)
butter for greasing
salt, pepper
600 g (1 lb 5 oz) prawns
120 g (4 oz) leeks

Shellfish sauce:
2 tbsp butter
1 tbsp flour
4 tbsp cognac or brandy
5 tbsp concentrated
shellfish stock (bottled)
50 ml (3 1/2 tbsp) white wine
400 ml (1 3/4 cups) whipping cream
salt, pepper

Method:

Begin with the sauce. Melt the butter in a saucepan. Stir in the flour. Pour in the cognac, concentrated shellfish stock, wine and cream. Bring to the boil, stirring. Allow it to simmer for 10 minutes, and add salt and pepper to taste. Keep warm.

Set the oven to 125°C (260°F). Grease 12 ramekins. Salt and pepper the fillets. Roll them up and place in the ramekins. Put onto a baking tray. Cook in the centre of the oven for about 15 minutes.

Peel prawns. Boil the leeks for a few minutes. Cut them lengthwise so that they look like wide ribbons.

Set aside the rolled fillets and pour the remaining juices into the sauce. Place the rolled fillets onto the ribbons of leek on warmed plates. Sprinkle the prawns over the top and pour over the sauce. For a hint of real luxury, garnish with slivers of truffle. Mashed potato goes well with this dish.

Tip: Sole which is prepared in one piece gets extra flavour from the bones. It is not particularly difficult to do, but to feed six people a large oven is needed. This dish is quite spectacular when decorated with the fish skeleton.

Method: Remove the heads and fins from 6 sole. Lay the fish in a greased dish, lightly covered with chopped shallots and well rinsed parsley stalks. Pour over around 200 ml (1 cup) of white wine. Cover with greaseproof paper and bake in the oven at 125°C (260°F) until the fillets come away from the bones. Sieve the juices. Peel away the fillets, and rinse the bones. Cook the sauce as described above but replace the wine with 100 ml (7 tbsp) fish stock. Take 100 ml (7 tbsp) of the liquid and make a white sauce using 150 g (5 oz) peeled prawns, a little dill and cornflour or thickening agent such as Maizena. Arrange the fillets on warmed plates with the sauce between them. Dip the fish skeleton into paprika and crown with this. Pour sauce around the edges. Garnish with the truffle slivers and possibly some green vegetables.

Dessert 1931

Curaçao Parfait Soufflé

Serves 6

8 egg yolks
100 ml (7 tbsp) Curaçao orange liqueur
100 ml (7 tbsp) sugar
the grated rind of an orange
500 ml (2 1/4 cups) whipping cream

Method:

Mix together the egg yolks, liqueur and sugar in a pan. Heat whilst whisking until it becomes thick and creamy. Remove from the heat and whisk until the cream cools.

Peel away the rind of the orange taking care to avoid the pith, then cut into thin strips. Blanch and allow to cool.

Whisk the cream and add to the egg mixture. Stir in the grated orange rind.

Line the outside of 6 ramekins with baking paper so that 2 cm (1 inch) protrudes above the rim and stick the paper together with tape. Fill the dishes to the top of the paper with the parfait mixture. Freeze for at least 4 hours.

Take away the baking paper and you have a parfait* which looks like a soufflé. Refrigerate for about 30 minutes before serving. Serve with, for example, almond biscuits or petits fours.

*Parfait means perfect, and here refers to perfect ice cream. It is smooth and creamy and very good.

Potatoes at the Banquet Table

Ever since the middle of the 19th century, potatoes have had their place on the Swedish dinner table for everyday meals as well as for special occasions. Often we are simply talking of new potatoes, boiled in their skins with dill.

Different types of potato dishes are suitable for special occasions. The choice of potato varieties is dependent on the method of preparation. Floury or firm. White or yellow inside. Hard potatoes are best for baking or frying or cutting into segments whilst soft ones are better for mashing or creaming. The seasons determine what is available in the shops.

At large gatherings, unpeeled potatoes are not really an option. During the war years boiling potatoes that had been peeled was forbidden in restaurants. The City Hall asked for a special exemption from this rule when there was a banquet for 300 people, using the argument:

"Having the staff peel the potatoes after they were cooked, but before they were served, would be impractical because of the large number of guests."

The Department of Food rejected the request.

Potatoes at the Banquet Table

Potato Swirls

Serves 6

1 1/2 kg (3 1/3 lb) potatoes
4–5 egg yolks
50 ml (3 1/2 tbsp) virgin olive oil
50 ml (3 1/2 tbsp) finely
grated horseradish
1 tsp salt
a pinch of white pepper

Method:

Set oven at 225°C (440°F). Peel and boil the potatoes in lightly salted water. Drain, mash or cream the potatoes. Stir in the egg yolks, olive oil and horseradish. Add salt and pepper to taste.

Pipe high potato swirls onto a greased baking tray. This first part of the recipe can all be prepared in advance.

Bake the swirls for about 10 minutes until golden brown.

Potatoes at the Banquet Table

Potatoes with Ginger

Serves 6

Method:

1 kg (2 lb) peeled potatoes
5 egg yolks
3 tbsp olive oil
2 tbsp dried ginger or about
30 g (1 oz) freshly grated root ginger
salt, pepper
optional freshly grated or
dried powdered nutmeg
potato flour and butter for frying

Cook and mash the potatoes. Mix in the egg yolks and olive oil. Add the spices. Roll the mixture up inside oiled greaseproof paper to about 4 cm (1 1/2 inches) in diameter. Leave to stand for at least 3 hours in the refrigerator.

Cut roll into 1/2 cm (1/4 inch) thick slices. Dip into the potato flour.

Fry the slices in butter until golden brown on both sides.

Easy Potato Bake

Serves 6

Method:

1 1/2 kg (3 1/3 lb) peeled potatoes
2 small onions
3 cloves of garlic
400 ml (1 3/4 cups) full cream milk
salt, pepper
grated cheese
butter

Cut the peeled potatoes into 3–4 mm (1/8 inch) thick slices.

Finely chop the onion and garlic and fry in the butter. Pour in the full cream milk. Remove from the heat. Add the potatoes. Simmer for about 10 minutes. Stir the bottom of the pan from time to time. Add salt and pepper.

Transfer to an ovenproof dish. Sprinkle over the grated cheese. Refrigerate until about 15 minutes before serving.

Bake at 200°C (400°F) until it turns nice and brown on top.

Potato Bake is a good dinner party dish as it can be prepared the day before.

Potatoes at the Banquet Table

Massenet Potatoes

Serves 6

Method:

900 g (2 lb) peeled potatoes
50 g (3 tbsp) butter
salt, white pepper
2 tbsp spring onions
cut into strips or leeks

Cut the potatoes into strips. Put them into cold water for a few minutes.

Drain the potatoes and dry them well.

Fry the potatoes in plenty of butter until they are golden brown and almost cooked through. Season with salt and pepper.

Grease 6 ovenproof baking dishes. Press the potatoes down into them. The recipe up to this point can be prepared a day in advance.

Just before serving, set the oven to 200°C (400°F). Heat up the potatoes for about 10 minutes. Then remove them and garnish with strips of spring onion or leek.

Potatoes at the Banquet Table

Lyonnaise Potatoes

Serves 6

Method:

1 1/4 kg (2 1/2 lb) potatoes
2 red onions
3 tbsp butter
2 tbsp sugar
50 ml (3 1/2 tbsp) red wine vinegar
salt, pepper

Peel and slice the potatoes into 1/2-cm (1/4 inch) thick slices. Peel and cut the onions into segments.

Fry the potatoes in 2 tbsp butter until golden brown and soft but still slightly al dente.

Fry the onions in the rest of the butter. Add the sugar and the vinegar. Stir and then cook gently for a few minutes.

Mix the onions with the potatoes. Add salt and pepper to taste.

Crispy Fried Potatoes

Serves 6

Method:

1 1/2 kg (3 1/3 lb) potatoes (firm variety)
50–100 ml (3–7 tbsp) cooking oil
3 tbsp butter
salt, pepper

Peel and slice the potatoes into wafer-thin slices. Rinse them in cold water, drain, and then dry them off with a clean tea towel until completely dry.

Fry the potatoes in batches in oil until they are crispy. Finally fry them in a knob of butter and salt and pepper them.

AFTER THE WAR YEARS, EUROPE BEGAN TO
GET BACK ON ITS FEET. DIOR INTRODUCED
THE WASP WAIST, WHICH WOULD REMAIN
A CLASSIC DESIGN IN THE FASHION WORLD
FOR A LONG TIME.

1947

George Marshall devised a plan of economic aid for war-torn Europe. He was later awarded the Nobel Peace Prize for his contribution. The first transistor was built at Bell Labs. Thor Heyerdahl sailed to Polynesia on the Kon-tiki raft.

The eminent English physicist, *Sir Edward V. Appleton*, received the Nobel Prize for his research into the ionosphere and the discovery of the Appleton layer, which makes global radio traffic possible. The Nobel Prize for Chemistry went to another famous Briton, *Sir Robert Robinson*, who synthesised and identified the chemical structure of alkaloids, including morphine and strychnine.

The Nobel Prize for Medicine was shared by the Austrian-American couple, *Carl F. Cori* and *Gerty T. Cori*, and the Argentinian, *Bernardo Houssay*, for their work on metabolic chemistry.

The great French writer, *André Gide*, was awarded the Nobel Prize for Literature for his novels, plays and documentaries, characterised by a certain nonconformity and acute psychological insight.

The Nobel Peace Prize went to the Quaker organisations, *The American Friends Service Committee* and *The Friends Service Council*. They worked tirelessly to help people affected by poverty and war.

1947

CLOSE TO NATURE WITH FLOWERS AND LEAVES, ALL THAT IS ALIVE AND WILD. A SPARKLING WINE AND A RIPPLING STREAM.

First Course 1947
Light Buffet with Canapés

Serving a buffet platter with small canapés is a pleasant way to combine an apéritif and appetisers. If you do not wish to make so many different sorts, you can choose, for example, three sorts and double the quantity for those.

Rolls of thin unleavened bread stuffed with
Skagen (seafood and vegetable) medley
Stir 1 tsp finely chopped dill, 1 tsp grated horseradish and 1 tsp finely chopped red onion into 2 tbsp of mayonnaise. Chop 75 g (2 1/2 oz) of peeled prawns and add to the mayonnaise. Spread the mixture onto a slice of soft, square, thin, unleavened bread. Roll it up like a Swiss roll. Just before serving, cut the roll into 6 pieces. Garnish them with 2 tbsp trout roe.

Royal Canapé
Whisk 50 ml (3 1/2 tbsp) crème fraîche until it stiffens. Season to taste with 2 tsp grated horseradish, a drop of vinegar essence and a pinch of sugar. Take two or three slices of a white tin loaf and cut out six circles about 5 cm (2 inches) in diameter. Butter them. Fold six large thin slices of smoked salmon into rose shapes. Place them on the circles of bread. Pipe the crème fraîche onto them or simply drop a spoonful on top. Garnish with a large prawn.

Cheese Canapé
Mix 150 g (5 oz) of Roquefort cheese with 50 ml (3 1/2 tbsp) mango chutney (finely chop the pieces of mango fruit if necessary). Take 6 slices of dark rye bread and cut out 6 circles about 5 cm (2 inches) in diameter. Pipe the creamy cheese onto the circles. Garnish each with a walnut.

Sandwich à la Knaust
Mix 2 tbsp grated horseradish with 100 ml (1/2 cup) cheese and horseradish spread. Spread half of the mixture onto 2 slices of long white open sandwich bread and the rest onto 2 equally large slices of dark rye bread (cut bread lengthways). Divide 4 slices of smoked venison and 3 tbsp finely diced gherkins onto the light bread and 4 slices of smoked salmon and 2 tbsp finely chopped dill onto the dark bread. Put the slices of bread together so that the light and dark bread alternate. Wrap in damp greaseproof paper and press down using a gentle weight. Cut off the crusts and slice thinly just before serving.

Gentleman's (anchovy and egg) medley on dark bread
Hard boil 3 eggs. Cool, shell and chop them. Mix carefully with 5 finely chopped anchovy fillets, 1 tsp mildly smoked caviar, 2 tbsp finely chopped red onion, 1 tbsp finely chopped chives and 1 tsp finely chopped dill. Take 6 slices of dark rye bread and cut out 6 circles about 5 cm (2 inches) in diameter. Spread the gentleman's medley onto the bread and garnish with a little cress.

Mini steak tartare with whitefish roe
Mince 200 g (1/2 lb) beef fillet steak. Add 1 egg yolk. Then stir in 2 tbsp finely chopped red onion, 2 tbsp finely chopped beetroot, and 2 tbsp capers. Add salt and pepper. Take a few slices of white tin loaf and cut out 6 circles 5 cm (2 inches) in diameter. Spread the meat mixture onto them. Garnish with about 30 g (1 oz) whitefish roe and 1 tbsp finely chopped red onion.

Main Course 1947

Roast Chicken Breast with Root Vegetables and Bacon

Serves 6

6 chicken breasts, each 140–150 g (5 oz)
salt, pepper

Root vegetable medley:
300 g (10 oz) celery stalks
4 shallots
150 g (5 oz) navets
150 g (5 oz) carrots
6 streaky bacon slices
2 tbsp butter
salt, pepper

Tarragon sauce:
half an onion
2 tbsp butter
1 tbsp dried tarragon
1 tbsp plain flour
100 ml (7 tbsp) red wine
300 ml (1 1/3 cups) whipping cream
4 tbsp concentrated
veal stock (bottled)
a pinch of sugar
2 tbsp French mustard
2 tbsp chopped parsley

Method:

Begin with the sauce. Finely chop the onion. Fry it in the butter and tarragon. Sprinkle over the flour. Stir in the wine, cream, veal stock and sugar. Cook for a few minutes. Add mustard to taste. Keep warm until the rest of the dish is ready.

Set the oven at 110°C (230°F). Brown the chicken breast all over and add salt and pepper. Roast for 10–15 minutes in the oven. Remove and wrap in greaseproof paper, then allow to rest for 5–10 minutes before cutting into slices.

Cut the celery stalks into pieces. Boil in lightly salted water until they are soft but still al dente. Peel the onion, navets and carrot. Chop the onion and cut the other vegetables into fine cubes. Cut the bacon into cubes too and fry in its own fat until crispy. Add onion, navets and carrot. Fry these in butter until soft. Add salt and pepper to taste. Mix with the celery.

Slice the chicken breast and arrange next to the root vegetables on warmed plates. Put the chopped parsley into the sauce and arrange this around the meat.

Dessert 1947

Stewed Apples on a Puff Pastry Base with Vanilla Custard

Serves 6

3 sheets of puff pastry
1 egg for glazing

Stewed Apples:
3 apples, preferably hard ones
such as Granny Smiths
50 ml (3 1/2 tbsp) lime cordial
2 tbsp brown sugar
a pinch of ground cinnamon
100 ml (1/2 cup) raisins,
preferably small sultana raisins
1/2 tbsp potato flour dissolved
in 1 tbsp lime cordial

Sauce:
1 packet of powdered custard
200 ml (1 cup) milk
50 ml (3 1/2 tbsp) crème fraîche

Method:

Set the oven at 175°C (350°F). Divide the puff pastry sheets into 6 pieces. Lay them on a baking tray covered with baking paper. Lightly beat the egg and glaze the pastry pieces. Bake for 7–8 minutes until the dough has risen and has turned golden brown in colour. Remove and allow to cool.

Make up the custard from the powder and milk following the directions on the packet. When it has thickened and cooled, whisk in the crème fraîche and refrigerate.

Peel and core the apples, then cut into cubes. Heat the lime cordial, sugar and cinnamon. Add the apple cubes and raisins. Cook until the apples are as soft as you would like them. Whisk together the potato flour and lime cordial mixture. Add it gradually, stirring constantly, until it becomes like syrup. Allow to cool.

Cut the puff pastry pieces horizontally across the middle. Arrange the bottom halves on the plates. Spoon over the apple mixture and the sauce. Place the top halves on top. A scoop of ice cream makes this dish even more delicious.

Tip: A fresh vanilla custard is not particularly difficult to make and for a special occasion, it can be worth while doing so. Method: Whisk 3 egg yolks with 100 ml (7 tbsp) sugar. Bring 100 ml (7 tbsp) milk and 150 ml (2/3 cup) whipping cream to the boil with a vanilla pod split in half. Whisk the cream and milk into the eggs and sugar mixture. Pour all of it into a pan and heat to simmering point. Dip 3 gelatine leaves into cold water for 5 minutes. Remove the leaves and squeeze out the liquid. Stir into the sauce so that they melt. Leave to cool. Take out the vanilla pod before serving.

With a Taste for the Good Things in Life

In 1954, the Nobel Prize for Literature was given to Ernest Hemingway,

*"for his mastery of the art of narrative, most recently demonstrated in
The Old Man and the Sea, and for the influence that he has exerted
on contemporary style".*

Throughout the whole of his professional life, Hemingway worked both as a writer and as a journalist in the field. There are many descriptions of dramatic events, which were penned by him.

Hemingway was not just known for his skill as an author, but also for his taste for the good things in life, including food and drink. However he was unable to enjoy the smoked rainbow trout and fillet of beef which was served at the Nobel Banquet in 1954, as he was forced to decline the invitation due to ill health.

When Hemingway chose to end his life by his own hand, he left behind him not only great literary works of art, but also anecdotes and several recipes for drinks.

IT CAME AS A GREAT SURPRISE TO LITERARY CIRCLES WHEN
HEMINGWAY PUBLISHED *THE OLD MAN AND THE SEA* IN 1952.
MANY PEOPLE BELIEVED HIS DAYS OF WRITING FICTION WERE
OVER, AFTER HIS YEARS AS A WAR CORRESPONDENT.

HEMINGWAY'S FAVOURITE DRINK
— A MIXTURE OF 1 PART RUM, 1 PART
LIME CORDIAL AND CRUSHED ICE
TOPPED UP WITH FRUIT SODA AND
A SPRIG OF MINT.

ALMOST 200 BOTTLES OF CHAMPAGNE ARE NEEDED TO FILL THE
GLASSES DURING A NOBEL BANQUET.

FOR A FEW YEARS CHAMPAGNE WAS REPLACED BY ORDINARY WINE,
BUT TODAY ITS PLACE IS SECURE.

Champagne, that drink where each bottle contains more than 40 million magic bubbles, has been on the Nobel menu right from the start; it was served at the very first banquet at the Grand Hôtel in 1901.

"Champagne should be cold, dry and free."
SIR WINSTON CHURCHILL

Author, statesman and connoisseur of champagne are all titles that can be applied to Sir Winston Churchill. He enjoyed a bottle of champagne daily and when he died, the champagne producer *Pol Roger* put a black mourning border on the labels. Today their prestigious champagne bears the name *Cuvée Sir Winston Churchill.*

The Swedish Academy awarded Sir Winston Churchill the Nobel Prize for Literature in 1953,

*"for his masterful portrayal of historical and biographical description,
as well as for his brilliant oratory in defending exalted human values".*

The laureate himself was unable to be in Stockholm but was represented by his wife, Lady Clementine. The students who were present at the banquet paid tribute to Churchill by singing *"Oh, my darling Clementine".*

OVER THE YEARS THE TASK OF PROVIDING THE NOBEL BANQUET WITH THIS GREAT DRINK HAS PASSED BETWEEN THE VARIOUS MAJOR CHAMPAGNE HOUSES IN ÉPERNAY.

AS SIR WINSTON CHURCHILL PUT IT "THE MOST DRINK-ABLE ADDRESS IN THE WORLD".

1954

The first portable transistor radio was launched. Tetra Pak, an important product for modern food distribution, was developed. Audrey Hepburn starred in the film *Roman Holiday*, becoming a beauty symbol for teenage girls.

The Nobel Prize for Physics was shared by two Germans, *Max Born* and *Walther Bothe*, for their respective theoretical experimental contribution to quantum mechanics a quarter of a century earlier. The American, *Linus C. Pauling*, received the Nobel Prize for Chemistry for his discoveries of how molecules in chemicals bond.

The Nobel Prize for Medicine was shared by three American virologists from the children's hospital in Boston, *John F. Enders, Frederick C. Robbins* and *Thomas H. Weller.* Thanks to their method of cultivating the polio virus, the polio vaccine could be produced and the first mass inoculations could take place.

The legendary American author, journalist, war hero and game hunter, *Ernest Hemingway*, received the Nobel Prize for Literature, but ill health prevented him from coming to Stockholm.

The Nobel Peace Prize went to the *UNHCR*, the Office of the United Nations High Commissioner for Refugees, which had been set up in Geneva in 1951.

THE WINNER OF THE 1954 NOBEL PRIZE FOR CHEMISTRY,
LINUS PAULING, IS THE ONLY PERSON TO WIN THE NOBEL
PRIZE TWICE IN HIS OWN RIGHT(OTHERS HAVE SHARED
PRIZES). FURTHERMORE, HE HAS WON IN TWO DIFFERENT
CATEGORIES. HE WARNED REPEATEDLY OF THE
CONSEQUENCES OF ATOMIC WAR AND WAS AWARDED THE
NOBEL PEACE PRIZE IN 1962.

1954

Hot Smoked Rainbow Trout with Spinach and Chanterelle Mushroom Sauce

Serves 6

6 hot smoked rainbow trout fillets of 90 g (3 oz) each or one whole piece weighing around 450 g (1 lb)

Spinach and Chanterelle Mushroom sauce:
300 g (10 oz) fresh chanterelle mushrooms
200 g (7 oz) fresh spinach
2 shallots
2 tbsp butter
1 tsp flour
150 ml (2/3 cup) whipped cream
50 ml (3 1/2 tbsp) port wine
150 ml (2/3 cup) crème fraîche
salt, white pepper
a little finely chopped red onion to garnish

Method:

Remove any skin from the trout. If using a whole piece, divide it into 6 portions. Wash mushrooms and spinach.

Peel and finely chop the onion. Fry gently in butter together with the chanterelle mushrooms but without browning. Sprinkle the flour over. Stir it round. Pour over the cream and port wine. Cook for a few minutes. Add the crème fraîche and salt and pepper to taste. Finally add the spinach just before serving.

Pour the spinach and chanterelle mushroom sauce onto warmed plates. Arrange the fish on top. Garnish, if desired, with finely chopped red onion.

Grilled Fillet of Beef with Tagliatelle Vegetables and Red Wine Sauce

Serves 6

1 kg (2 lb) fillet of beef
salt, pepper

Tagliatelle vegetables:
400 g (1 lb) tagliatelle (pasta),
multi-coloured if possible
2 large carrots
400 g (1 lb) mushrooms
1 shallot
1 tsp truffle oil or cooking oil
1 tbsp flour
3 tbsp white port wine
200 ml (1 cup) crème fraîche
salt, pepper

Red wine sauce:
300 ml (1 1/3 cups) red wine
50 ml (3 1/2 tbsp) water
4 tbsp concentrated
veal stock (bottled)
2 bay leaves
1 tsp brown sugar
a pinch of white pepper
2 shallots
1 tbsp butter
1 tsp cornflour or thickening agent
such as Maizena + 2 tbsp red wine

Method:

Begin with the sauce. Bring the wine, water and veal stock to the boil with the bay leaves, brown sugar and white pepper. Allow to cook for 3 minutes. Remove the sauce from the heat and let the flavour of the herbs be extracted for about 15 minutes. Peel and finely chop the onion. Fry the onion until soft in butter but without browning. Pour the sauce over the fried onions. Thicken with the cornflour or equivalent dissolved in red wine. Bring to the boil and keep warm until served.

Set the oven at 110°C (230°F).

Tagliatelle vegetables. Cut thin slices of carrot lengthwise using either a cheese slice or a knife. Blanch.

Finely slice the mushrooms. Peel and finely chop the shallots. Fry in truffle oil until the liquid has evaporated, but without browning the mushrooms or onions. Sprinkle the flour over and stir. Add the port wine and crème fraîche. Bring to the boil and keep warm. It may be necessary to dilute with a little water.

Boil the pasta in lightly salted water until it is al dente. Add the carrot slices and pasta to the mushrooms in the pan. Stir and add salt and pepper to taste. Keep warm until it is served.

Cut the meat into 6 equally large pieces. Salt, pepper and sear the meat over a high heat on both sides. Put the pieces of meat in the oven until they go pink in the middle. This is at around 58°C (136°F). Preferably measure this using a meat thermometer.

Arrange the tagliatelle vegetables onto warmed plates. Place the meat on top and pour the sauce around. Fried parsley is an exciting garnish for this dish.

Dessert 1954

Green Pears with Pistachio Nut Ice Cream

Serves 6

6 small pears
1 vanilla pod
400 ml (1 3/4 cups) water
a drop of green food colouring
300 ml (1 1/3 cups) sugar
100 ml (1/2 cup) green Chartreuse (liqueur)
1 litre (4 1/2 cups) pistachio nut ice cream

Method:

Peel the pears but leave the stems on.

Halve the vanilla pod lengthwise. Scrape out the seeds into a pan. Lay the pod in the pan too. Pour in the water, food colouring, sugar and liqueur. Stir and bring to the boil.

Place the pears into the liquid and cook them until they are medium soft; there should still be some hardness left. Remove them from the liquid and leave the liquid to cool.

Return them to the liquid and leave to marinate for 1–2 days.

Measure 500 ml (2 1/4 cups) of the liquid. Boil rapidly until reduced to 200 ml (1 cup). The dish can be prepared in advance up to this point the day before the dinner.

Put the ice cream in the refrigerator a few hours before serving.

Scoop the ice cream out with a warmed spoon or ice cream scoop. Put onto the plates. Place the pears next to the ice cream and pour over a little of the liquid.

1969

In this year the front pages of the newspapers were filled with stories of space exploration. Apollo XI's landing on the moon and the Soviet Union's first docking between two manned spacecraft were perhaps the most important milestones.

The American, *Murray Gell-Mann*, received the Nobel Prize for Physics for his quark theory. The Nobel Prize for Chemistry was shared by an Englishman, *Sir Derek H. Barton*, and a Norwegian, *Odd Hassel*, for their contribution to the ideas about the conformation of organic molecular structure.

The German-American molecular biologist, *Max Delbrück*, together with his colleagues, *Alfred D. Hershey* and *Salvador Luria*, received the Nobel Prize for Medicine for pioneering studies into viruses and their genetic structure, primarily the bacteriophage.

The Nobel Prize for Literature went to the Irish playwright, *Samuel Beckett*, world famous for his play *Waiting for Godot*. Beckett, who was shy of publicity, declined to attend.

The United Nations' *International Labour Organisation* received the Nobel Peace Prize on its 50th anniversary. The Bank of Sweden's Nobel Memorial Prize for Economics was awarded for the first time and went to the Norwegian, *Ragnar Frisch*, and the Dutchman, *Jan Tinbergen*.

THE ASTRONAUT EDWIN "BUZZ" ALDRIN SETS FOOT ON THE MOON. THE TIMETABLE FOR 21ST JULY 1969 IS ON SCHEDULE DOWN TO THE LAST SECOND.

1969 STRONG COLOURS
MEET STRONG
DESIRES. OLD AND
NEW TOGETHER. THERE ARE NO RULES.

First Course 1969

Salmon and Avocado with White-fish Roe and Horseradish Sauce

Serves 6

12 thin slices of gravad lax
(raw spiced salmon), about 400 g (1 lb)
4 ripe avocados
150 g (5 oz) feta cheese
1 red onion

Dressing:
2 tbsp red wine vinegar
3 tbsp olive oil
a pinch of freshly ground black pepper

Whitefish roe and horseradish sauce:
200 ml (1 cup) soured cream
2 tbsp grated horseradish
2 tbsp finely snipped chives
1 tsp sugar
a drop of vinegar essence
60 g (2 oz) whitefish roe

Method:

Begin with the sauce. Mix everything together apart from the whitefish roe. Add this shortly before serving.

Halve and remove the stones from the avocados. Scoop out the avocado flesh and cut up half of the avocado into cubes. Cut the cheese into similar cubes. Peel and finely chop the onion. Chop half of the salmon. Mix these together. Whisk the ingredients for the dressing together. Stir the dressing into the mixture. Cut the remaining avocados into 18 thin segments.

Pile the mixture in the centre of the plate. Lay the salmon and avocado segments around it and encircle it with sauce.

Tip: Sprinkle a few drops of lime or lemon juice over the avocados so that they do not discolour so easily.

Stuffed Fillet of Beef with Madeira Sauce and Glazed Shallots

Serves 6

800 g (1 3/4 lb) lean fillet of beef
lard for frying
salt, pepper

Filling:
250 g (1/2 lb) finely minced beef
2 egg yolks
2 tbsp French mustard
2 tbsp capers
2 tbsp grated horseradish
50 ml (3 1/2 tbsp) finely chopped parsley
salt

Madeira sauce:
2 shallots
1 tbsp butter
1 tbsp brown sugar
200 ml (1 cup) red wine
150 ml (2/3 cup) madeira
100 ml (7 tbsp) water
4 tbsp concentrated
veal stock (bottled)
1 tsp balsamic vinegar
a pinch of white pepper
1 tbsp cornflour or thickening agent,
e.g. Maizena + 2 tbsp red wine

Glazed shallots:
24 shallots, about 500 g (1 lb)
2 tbsp butter
50 ml (3 1/2 tbsp) sugar
200 ml (1 cup) water or lager

Method:

Set the oven at 110°C (230°F). Mix together the meat and egg yolks. Add the mustard, capers, horseradish, parsley and salt.

Cut the fillet of beef lengthwise so that it looks like an unfolded roll. Spread the mince onto the fillet and roll up like a Swiss roll. Tie cotton thread around the beef so that it stays together.

Brown the meat in the fat. Season. Roast in the oven until the inner temperature reaches about 65°C (150°F) in the middle (preferably use a meat thermometer to measure this). Wrap the fillet in greaseproof paper and allow to rest until the other things are ready.

The sauce: Peel and finely chop the onion. Fry in butter in a saucepan. Add the brown sugar, red wine, madeira, water, veal stock, vinegar and pepper. Bring the sauce to the boil and then simmer for about 5 minutes. Dissolve the cornflour or equivalent in the red wine. Whisk it into the sauce. Bring to the boil. Keep warm. If the sauce seems too thick or too strong in taste, dilute it with a little water.

Peel the onions. Fry them in butter until they are golden in colour. Sprinkle the sugar over them and allow them to caramelize. Pour in the water/lager and cook until the onions are soft and the liquid has a syrup-like consistency.

Cut the meat into 1 cm (1/2 inch) thick slices. Arrange on warmed plates with the shallot onions and the sauce. Crispy fried potatoes go well with this dish. See the recipe on page 86.

Dessert 1969

Orange Sorbet with Red Grapefruit Salad

Serves 6

5–6 oranges
200 ml (1 cup) sugar
200 ml (1 cup) water
50 ml (3 1/2 tbsp) glucose
(available from chemists)
100 ml (7 tbsp) concentrated orange juice

Red grapefuit salad:
4 red grapefruits
1/2 vanilla pod
150 ml (2/3 cup) sugar
100 ml (7 tbsp) water
1 cinnamon stick
50 ml (3 1/2 tbsp) pistachio nuts

Method:

Halve and extract the juice from the oranges. Sieve it and measure 500 ml (2 cups). Mix the sugar and water in a pan. Add the glucose and extracted juice. Bring to the boil. Allow to cool. Add the concentrated orange juice. Put the mixture into an ice cream maker and switch it on until it is creamy. The temperature should be around −8°C (18°F).

Peel and cut the grapefruit segments between the layers of skin. Squeeze the juice from what is left of the grapefruit. Split the vanilla pod in half lengthwise. Scrape out the seeds into a pan. Put the pod in too and add sugar, water, cinnamon stick and the squeezed, sieved grapefruit juice. Bring to the boil then allow to stand for at least 6 hours to extract the flavour. Let the grapefruit segments lie in the juices for at least 15 minutes before serving.

Arrange the grapefruit segments with their juices on the plates. Use an ice cream scoop or spoon to place scoops of sorbet onto the grapefruit salad. Spread the pistachio nuts over the top.

Tip: This looks attractive garnished with thin blanched strips of grapefruit rind.

Pedestals AND FRUIT BASKETS FILLED WITH MODERN DECORATIONS.

Floral Tapestries and Individual Anemones

Lilies, orchids, Gerbera, gladioli and roses in striking colours. During the course of the Nobel celebrations, more than 23,000 flowers grace the awards ceremony at the Concert Hall and the banquet at the City Hall. Over the years the floral decorations have become more and more varied – from elaborate arrangements to single flowers, laid at random on every tablecloth.

Alfred Nobel spent his final years and ended his days at San Remo, a centre for flower cultivation on the Italian riviera. The mild climate was good for his health. Alfred's home, Villa Nobel, is today a museum, which is also used by Swedish-Italian joint projects in cultural and scientific studies.

As a tribute to his memory, every year the *Azienda di Promozione Turistica di Sanremo*, which promotes tourism in the Italian town, donates flowers, which adorn the Nobel celebrations. The flowers are carefully transported to Stockholm where professional florists create tasteful arrangements.

Majestic FULL OF STRENGTH AND LIFE.
A LILY IN WARM COLOURS.

Aubergine AND SAVOY CABBAGE ARRANGED WITH TULIPS AND ROSES.

Beauty FROM ALL LATITUDES
THROUGHOUT THE YEAR.

A Miracle
LITTLE THINGS CAN
MAKE THE DIFFERENCE.

Alone OR IN COMPANY.
A ROSE IS ALWAYS A ROSE.

INGMAR BERGMAN'S TV VERSION
OF MOZART'S "THE MAGIC FLUTE"
WAS A GREAT SUCCESS.

1975

Nouvelle cuisine has spread throughout Europe. The French chef Paul Bocuse, one of the originators of the idea, has received the Legion of Honour from President Giscard d'Estaing.

The Nobel Prize for Physics was shared by the Dane, *Aage Bohr*, the son of Niels Bohr, and the Americans, *Ben R. Mottelson* and *James Rainwater*, for their collective model of the atomic nucleus. The Nobel Prize for Chemistry went to *Sir John W. Cornforth*, of Australia, and *Vladimir Prelog*, of Switzerland, who charted the stereochemistry of enzyme catalyst reactions.

David Baltimore, Renato Dulbecco and *Howard M. Temin*, from the USA shared the Nobel Prize for Medicine for establishing how a retrovirus copies its RNA onto the host cells' DNA. The work is to have great significance a few years later when a previously unknown retrovirus, named HIV, is identified in San Francisco.

The headstrong Italian poet, *Eugenio Montale*, received the Nobel Prize for Literature and the Peace Prize went to the Soviet physicist, *Andrei Sakharov*.

The Soviet, *Leonid Kantorovich*, and *Tjalling C. Koopmans*, of the USA, shared the Economics Prize for their work involving optimal allocation of resources.

1975

CONTRASTS. HARD AND SOFT.
BLACK AND WHITE. WOOD MEETS STONE.

Fish and Shellfish in Aspic with Mustard Vinaigrette

Serves 6

550 g (1 1/4 lb) brill or other flat fish fillets
shellfish, e.g. 12 prawns or 6 lobster claws or crayfish tails
50 ml (3 1/2 tbsp) finely chopped dill
1 head of rocket

Aspic:
4 tbsp concentrated fish stock (bottled) e.g. anchovy essence
200 ml (1 cup) white wine
200 ml (1 cup) water
2 tbsp white wine vinegar
3 sprigs dill
3 bay leaves
5 gelatine leaves

Mustard Vinaigrette:
150 ml (2/3 cup) olive oil
2 tbsp red wine vinegar
1 tbsp Dijon mustard
1 tsp sugar
2 tbsp finely chopped dill

Method:

Set the oven at 110°C (230°F).

Begin with the aspic. Bring the fish stock, wine, water, vinegar, dill sprigs and bay leaves to the boil. Turn off the stove, but leave on the heat for 10 minutes to extract the flavour.

Soak the gelatine leaves for 5–10 minutes.

Sieve the aspic solution. Press any remaining moisture out of the gelatine leaves. Stir them into the aspic which should still be hot.

Divide the fish fillets into pieces. Layer the fish, shellfish and chopped dill into 6 individual moulds. Pour over the aspic solution. Put in the oven for 10–15 minutes. Remove and allow to cool. Refrigerate. This can be done 1–2 days in advance.

Mix the ingredients for the mustard vinaigrette.

Turn out the aspic moulds and place on a bed of rocket. Pour over the vinaigrette.

Aspic is the perfect party food, as it can be prepared 1 or 2 days in advance. The fish and shellfish which are included can naturally be varied according to taste or availability.

Main Course 1975

Roast Snow Goose with Mushroom Sauce and Beetroot

Serves 6

6 snow grouse (ptarmigan)
salt, pepper
oil for frying

Wild (Morel) mushroom sauce:
a grouse carcass
1 onion
1 carrot
1 celeriac
oil for frying
100 ml (7 tbsp) madeira
100 ml (7 tbsp) red wine
water
10 juniper berries
10 white pepper corns
2 bay leaves
4 tbsp concentrated
game stock (bottled)
1 tbsp cornflour or equivalent
thickening agent
e.g. Maizena + 2 tbsp red wine
100 g (3 1/2 oz) cleaned parboiled
wild mushrooms (Morel)
(or use dried if fresh not available)
2 tbsp butter for frying

Truffle-flavoured beetroot:
350 g (12 oz) fresh beetroot
2 tsp truffle oil
100 ml (1/2 cup) water
4 tbsp balsamic vinegar
4 tbsp sugar

Method:

Cut off the grouse breasts including both the meat and the bone. Break off the rump and discard. Cut the carcass into small pieces.

Peel and cut the vegetables into small pieces. Brown them with the carcass pieces in a frying pan. Then transfer to a thick bottomed casserole dish. Add the madeira and red wine. Pour on water to cover. Bring to the boil and remove scum. Add the herbs and spices and cook for 40 minutes.

Sieve the liquid and boil rapidly until it reduces by about half. Add the game stock. Dissolve the cornflour or equivalent in the wine. Pour this in gradually whilst stirring constantly. Fry the morel mushrooms in butter. Pour the sauce over and keep warm.

Set the oven at 100°C (210°F). Salt and pepper the grouse breasts. Brown them on both sides in a frying pan, then cook in the oven for another 5–10 minutes. Wrap the breasts in grease-proof paper and let them rest until the beetroots are ready.

Peel and slice the beetroots as thinly as possible, using a cheese slice or mandolin. Mix the truffle oil, water, balsamic vinegar and sugar in a pan. Bring to the boil. Cook the beetroot slices for 5–10 minutes in the truffle liquid. Save a little of this for glazing the beetroots when they are served.

Cut the grouse breast away from the bone and slice thinly. Lay it back onto the bone for shape. Serve on a bed of beetroot slices, and encircle with the morel sauce. This goes well with a mixed salad and, for example, Massenet potatoes. See the recipe on page 85.

Dessert 1975

Lingonberry Parfait with Berry Sauce and Almond Biscuits

Serves 6

6 egg yolks
500 ml (2 cups) whipping cream
100 ml (7 tbsp) sugar
150 g (5 oz) preserved raw lingonberries
2 tbsp lemon vodka

Berry sauce:
150 g (5 oz) frozen strawberries
2 tbsp sugar
50 g (1 1/2 oz) preserved raw lingonberries

Almond biscuits:
200 g (7 oz) marzipan
2 egg whites
whole almonds for decoration

Method:

Whisk the egg yolks and sugar in a bain marie* until they are frothy. Add the lingonberries. Whisk until stiff.

Remove the bain marie* from the heat and continue to whisk until the mixture has cooled. Add vodka to taste. Whisk the cream and fold in carefully. Fill individual dishes or one large one with the parfait mixture. Freeze for at least 6 hours.

The sauce. Mix the strawberries with the sugar. Strain through a fine sieve so that you have a smooth sauce. Add the preserved raw lingonberries. Refrigerate.

Set the oven at 200°C (400°F). Grate the marzipan using the fine side of the grater. Add the egg whites and stir until smooth. Pipe small swirls onto a greased baking tray. Garnish with whole almonds. Cook for 5–8 minutes. Allow the biscuits to cool.

Take the parfait out in good time and transfer to the refrigerator at least half an hour before serving. Cut into 6 pieces, or dip the individual dishes into hot water and turn out the parfaits. Serve with berry sauce and biscuits.

*Bain marie is an arrangement where you heat a large pan full of hot water and place a smaller bowl or pan containing your ingredients inside it. This gives a gentle heat, which never exceeds 100°C (212°F).

Behind the Scenes

From an event involving 150 guests, the Nobel Banquet has grown into an enormous dramatic spectacle and it has to be prepared for as such. The comparison with the opening night of a famous old play would not be far from the mark. A Shakespeare, Ibsen or Strindberg, where everyone already knows the plot. But the public likes to be charmed, seduced and surprised by some new unexpected angle. Both for the banquet and for the spectacle, it is a question of working with a particular script, finding dramatic peaks, choosing performers, stage design, costumes, rehearsals and music. It is also the opening night.

The event has developed through the years, but it can still be said that it has found its own level, as there are a number of restrictions involving the design of the hall, the seating plan and the ceremony. But there is, of course, also room for creativity and innovation.

The Nobel menus are without exaggeration one of the evening's main attractions – a dramatic highlight, if you will. There is also, of course, only a limited number who have the chance to create such a menu. The City Hall caterers now divide the task, which is a great honour, between selected guest chefs. The broad outlines are fairly simple. The meal must be varied and Scandinavian in character. The chefs must also bear in mind that the kitchen is located four floors above the Blue Hall, so the food must be able to be transported before it is served to the guests.

BEHIND A NOBEL BANQUET LIE MONTHS OF
PREPARATIONS. LARS-GÖRAN ANDERSSON AND
STEFAN JOHNSON PLAN THE 1998 MENU.

In September three suggested menus are prepared for testing and tasting. Members of the Nobel Foundation take seat at the previously laid table, and eat, drink and discuss the food. Agreement is reached about which of the suggested menus is to be served and the menu is then kept secret until the actual day of the Nobel Banquet.

A coveted assignment

Working at the Nobel Banquet is coveted, although it could be compared to a strictly disciplined marathon performance. Many staff return year after year and there are waiters who have taken part more than 25 times.

It is in early autumn that the decisions are made as to who will work at the Nobel Banquet. An ability to work well in a team as well as skill in the art of serving are naturally two important criteria for employment. For waiting staff, it is important to be able to balance one of the serving platters and serve in front of TV cameras and millions of viewers.

Every banquet needs a catering manager, banqueting hall manager, head chef, eight head waiters, 210 waiters and waitresses, five wine waiters, 20 cooks and a similar number again responsible for washing up and transporting the food. In addition, there are reserves in case anyone falls ill or is too nervous to be able to serve.

Ready on schedule

Three days before the big day, preparations begin in the kitchen. Everyone works according to a strict schedule and the head chef gratefully ticks off

THE NOBEL BANQUET IS AN EXACTING AND COVETED TASK.
MANY OF THE STAFF RETURN YEAR AFTER YEAR.

IN THE KITCHEN THE PRACTICAL PREPARATIONS
BEGIN THREE DAYS BEFORE THE BANQUET.

each finished item on his list. Delivery vans unload one after another; everything is brought under control and stored where it should go.

Food is cut up, checked, peeled, fried, seasoned and tasted. Each dish is prepared down to the last detail so that it can be quickly finished off when the guests arrive.

The shopping list for the 1,268 covers is, to say the least, impressive. One year it included 2,692 pigeon breasts, 475 lobster tails, 100 kilos of potatoes, 70 litres of sweet and sour raspberry vinegar sauce, 67 kilos of Jerusalem artichokes, 53 kilos of Philadelphia cheese, 45 kilos of lightly smoked salmon plus a few other items…

The penultimate day. The schedule is packed. 65 tables are laid out in their exact positions in the Blue Hall. 470 metres of tablecloth are rolled out and 30 people wearing white gloves begin the time-consuming task of laying the tables. The Nobel dinner service consisting of 6,730 pieces of porcelain, 5,384 glasses, and 9,422 pieces of cutlery is laid out. The six obelisks, which represent the prizes, are set out. The same care is taken for each place setting, be it at the table of honour or the table reserved for students of various Swedish universities who attend the meal.

Florists and their assistants arrange a sea of flowers and exotic fruit. The orchestra rehearses, entertainers rehearse their various entrances and acts. All movements are carefully noted. In the kitchen, concentration on the work in hand is intensifying. Before the lights are switched off for the night, everything must be ready before the next day's minute by minute schedule.

Serving staff rehearse. The banqueting manager stands, stopwatch in hand,

CARL DE GEER BOUGHT THE FRENCH GOLD CANDELABRAS IN THE MID 1850S AND THEY HAVE GRACED MANY A SWEDISH DELEGATION'S TABLE THROUGHOUT EUROPE BEFORE EMBELLISHING THE CITY HALL.

overseeing all the movements between tables. A few seconds can be saved here and there. The ice cream parade, one of the evening's highlights, is served within three minutes. The time is calculated from the moment when the first waiter appears in the doorway until the last one reaches his table. All other courses take two minutes to serve.

In today's media-driven world, it is easy to believe that the split-second timing is dictated by the live television schedules and the sacrosanct commercial breaks being shown around the world, but that is not the case. It is simply a question of the guests being served the best possible quality food.

To achieve this, everyone has to work to a schedule based on minutes. Included in this time scale are the speeches, and the speaker who does not keep to time can hold up 210 waiters and waitresses behind the scenes holding steaming serving platters.

One last check. Everything is in its place before the big day. The lights are turned off in the Blue Hall. From the Golden Hall the echo of the dance band's final note is heard.

The general rehearsal is over. The actual performance can begin.

JOHN LENNON IS SHOT
DEAD IN NEW YORK.

1980

Björn Borg won his fifth Wimbledon title after what was probably his most successful season. Another great Alfred passed away – Alfred Hitchcock. If there were a Nobel Prize for Films, he would have been an obvious candidate.

James W. Cronin and *Val L. Fitch*, USA, received the Nobel Prize for Physics for discovering a rare exception to the rules of interaction for matter and antimatter. The Briton, *Frederick Sanger*, and the Americans, *Walter Gilbert* and *Paul Berg*, were the winners of the Nobel Prize for Chemistry for crucial progress in the field of genetic engineering.

The Nobel Prize for Medicine was shared by *Baruj Benacerraf*, a Venezuelan-born American, *Jean Dausset*, from France, and *George D. Snell*, from the USA, for charting the genetic reasons behind rejection problems during transplants.

The Polish-American writer, *Czeslaw Milosz*, once a resistance fighter in the ghettos of Warsaw, received the Nobel Prize for Literature; he has been called the greatest poet of our time.

The Nobel Peace Prize was given to the Argentinian sculptor, *Adolfo Pérez Esquivel*, who fought for human rights during the military junta's dictatorship.

The Nobel Prize for Economics went to *Lawrence R. Klein*, from the USA, for his work with state of the market models and economic analysis.

First Course 1980

Cold Smoked Salmon on a Bed of Spinach with Poached Egg

Serves 6

12 thin slices of cold smoked salmon, weighing about 500 g (1 lb)

Creamed spinach:
1 packet of frozen spinach leaves weighing 250 g (1/2 lb)
2 shallots
2 tbsp butter
200 ml (1 cup) crème fraîche
salt, white pepper

Poached eggs:
6 eggs
2 litres (9 cups) water
50 ml (3 1/2 tbsp) vinegar essence
2 tbsp salt

Method:

Begin with the eggs. Boil the water, vinegar and salt in a wide stainless pan. Lower the heat so that the water is just simmering. Break an egg into a coffee cup. Let it carefully glide into the water. Hold the egg together with two wooden spoons. Poach for no more than 3 minutes. Carefully transfer the egg into cold water. Repeat with the other eggs. Experienced cooks can put several in together at a time. Can be prepared in good time before the party.

Squeeze the moisture out of the defrosted spinach. Peel and finely chop the onion. Fry the onion in butter until it is transparent. Add the spinach and crème fraîche and heat through. Add salt and pepper to taste. Keep warm.

Bring the water to the boil in a wide pan. Lower the heat so that it just simmers. Carefully lower in the poached eggs and heat up until they are warm.

Arrange the creamed spinach on warmed plates. Lay the salmon slices on top and put the egg alongside. A little freshly ground black pepper adds to the flavour.

Main Course 1980

Fillet of Venison with Chanterelle Mushrooms and Aquavit Sauce

Serves 6

1 kg (2 lb) trimmed venison fillet (preferably an outer cut of meat)
salt, pepper

Chanterelle Mushrooms:
600 g (1 1/3 lb) fresh, washed chanterelle mushrooms (reddish yellow horns of plenty or funnel chanterelles)
1 onion
50 g (1 1/2 oz) carrots
50 g (1 1/2 oz) green beans
2 tbsp butter
salt, pepper

Aquavit sauce:
300 ml (1 1/3 cups) whipping cream
100 ml (7 tbsp) red wine
4 tbsp concentrated game stock (bottled)
10 crushed juniper berries
2 bay leaves
2 shallot onions
2 tbsp butter
1 tbsp flour
a pinch of black pepper
2 tbsp aquavit

Method:

Begin with the sauce. Heat the cream, wine and game stock along with the juniper berries and bay leaves. Reduce the heat and allow to stand and extract the flavour for 15–20 minutes.

Set the oven at 100°C (210°F). Sear the venison fillet. Add salt and pepper and then cook in the oven until the inner temperature reaches about 58°C (136°F) (preferably measure using a meat thermometer). Remove and wrap in greaseproof paper. Allow to rest until everything else is ready.

Peel and finely chop the shallot for the sauce. Fry it in butter but without browning. Sprinkle the flour over it and stir. Pour over the sauce and add black pepper and aquavit to taste. Keep warm.

Cut up any of the mushrooms that are too big. Peel and finely chop the onion. Finely cube the carrot; cut the beans up into small lengths.

Fry the mushrooms in butter. Add the chopped onion, fry for a few minutes, then add the cubed carrot. Fry a little more, then stir in the beans. Add salt and pepper to taste. Keep warm.

Arrange the mushroom mixture on warmed plates. Pour over the sauce. Cut the fillets into thin slices and lay on top of the mushrooms. This dish goes well with Lyonnaise potatoes. See the recipe on page 86.

Tip: If the sauce is too thick or strong, dilute slightly.

Dessert 1980

Kiwi Fruit Sorbet with Fruit in a Beer Marinade

Serves 6

Kiwi fruit sorbet:
6–7 kiwi fruits, about 400 g (1 lb)
150 ml (2/3 cup) sugar
150 ml (2/3 cup) water
zest of 1/2 a lime

Fruit for marinating:
3 kiwi fruits
2 mangos (ripe)
18 strawberries

Beer marinade:
2 gelatine leaves
3 oranges
1 1/2 lemons
1/2 vanilla pod
200 ml (1 cup) sugar
300 ml (1 1/3 cups) wheat beer

Method:

Begin with the sorbet. Peel, cut and then mash the kiwi fruit into a pulp. Push through a sieve. Measure 300 ml (1 1/3 cups). Bring the water and sugar to the boil. Strip the zest from the lime. Put this and the sugar solution in with the kiwi pulp. Pour this into an ice cream maker. Run until a creamy sorbet consistency is reached. Freeze for at least 6 hours.

Dip the gelatine leaves into cold water for 5 minutes. Peel off the zest of 1 orange, avoiding the pith. Cut the zest into thin strips. Squeeze the juice from both the orange and the lemon. Cut the vanilla pod in half. Scrape out the seeds and put them into a pan along with the rest of the pod. Add the orange juice and zest, lemon juice, sugar and wheat beer. Heat the liquid and remove any scum.

Press any moisture out of the gelatine leaves. Dissolve them in the hot liquid. Peel and stone the fruit. Cut into pieces. Marinate in the liquid for several hours.

Serve fruit and marinade. Place a scoop of kiwi sorbet on top.

Tip: Make up this recipe then use it as a basis for others.
1. Kiwi sorbet with fresh fruit and beer sabayon: Cut the fruit into small pieces, or slices. As an accompaniment, make a good sabayon sauce: Mix 200 ml (1 cup) sugar, 7 egg yolks, and the zest and juice of one lime with 300 ml (1 1/3 cups) fruit beer (raspberry, cherry or black or red currant) in a pan. Heat in a bain marie whilst whisking until the mixture thickens. Remove from the heat and continue to whisk until it has cooled. The sauce can be served hot or cold. The cold sauce can be prepared well in advance. Shortly before serving, fold 150 ml (2/3 cup) whipped cream into the sauce.
2. Kiwi sorbet with chocolate grilled fruit: Cut the fruit into small pieces/slices. Divide the fruit between 6 ovenproof plates. Grate 120 g (4 oz) of white chocolate block over the fruit. Grill quickly on high or brown in a hot oven. Serve immediately with kiwi fruit sorbet.

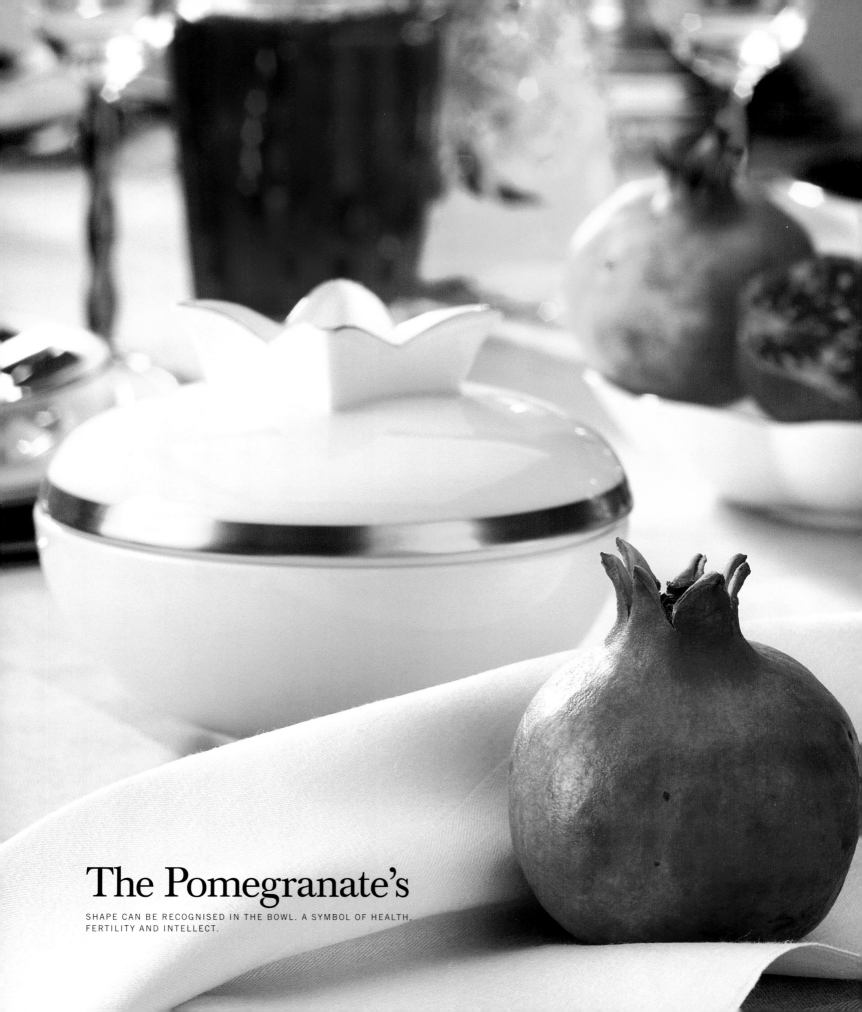

The Pomegranate's

SHAPE CAN BE RECOGNISED IN THE BOWL. A SYMBOL OF HEALTH,
FERTILITY AND INTELLECT.

Nobel Jubilee

Jubilees are a stimulating challenge for every event organiser. Guests have high expectations and the desire to give them an unforgettable experience is strong.

In other words, it is easy to understand how much rested on the shoulders of the Nobel Foundation's chief executive, Stig Ramel, prior to the Nobel Prizes' 90th anniversary in 1991. A celebration of this size and dignity is of course not just down to the work of one person. He therefore consulted with Åke Livstedt, an art historian, and Magnus Silverhielm, an architect. The pair were given the task of coming up with inspirational ideas for the jubilee.

One of their suggestions had that obvious simplicity, which characterises great ideas when they are well presented. The suggestion can be summarised as follows: the Nobel Banquet would have its own dinner service, jointly produced by skilled Swedish craftsmen and successful Swedish companies, using internationally renowned designers.

Karin Björquist created the fantastic, stimulating and bold porcelain. She found inspiration in the Japanese art of table decoration and in 18th century rococo. The service's pieces are hand decorated in gold, bright green, yellow and blue. The manufacturer is Hackman Rörstrand.

The glasses have particulary evocative shapes and colours, that set the mind thinking. They are designed by Gunnar Cyrén and produced by Orrefors. Each glass is made by hand from unleaded crystal and the

The Shapes

AND COLOURS IN THE NOBEL DINNER SERVICE ARE OFTEN TALKING POINTS, JUST LIKE THE CONVERSATION PIECES WHICH WERE PLACED ON THE TABLE IN THE PAST TO KEEP THE CONVERSATION ALIVE DURING LONG DINNERS.

stems are either blue or green, or hand-painted in 22 carat gold. The choice of colours is a tribute to the Swedish glass master craftsman Simon Gate.

Gunnar Cyrén even gave a distinctive shape to the cutlery, which is produced by Gense. It is made from silver, stainless steel or gold plated steel and is inspired by Karl Johan XIV's table silver. Despite the classical muse, playfulness peeps out in the creation of the original fish knives.

The tablecloth and serviettes add the perfect finishing touch to the Nobel Banquet table. They supply the discreet background, which the original and brightly coloured porcelain and glass need, to show them off to their full advantage. The designer is Ingrid Dessau. She has combined modern design and techniques with the traditional methods used by the Klässbol Linneväveri. The tablecloth is woven in a simply patterned linen fabric and the serviettes are made from damask. Using computer technology a portrait of Alfred Nobel himself is woven into one of the corners.

The Nobel dinner service is an impressive piece of work, of which the man it was named after would no doubt be justifiably proud, because it is, in a way, a reflection of his own unconventional methods and diverse skills.

Spring

VIVALDI'S "FOUR SEASONS" WOULD SUIT THIS ROMANTIC DINNER WELL. THE CHANGING SEASONS WERE ALSO ONE OF THE SOURCES OF INSPIRATION FOR THE DESIGNER KARIN BJÖRQUIST.

Winter

THE BLUE COLOUR SYMBOLISES THE SWEDISH WINTER. THIS TABLE SETTING IS AT THE ICE HOTEL IN JUKKASJÄRVI. IT IS OPEN WHEN THE TEMPERATURE IS BELOW 0°C.

Champagne BREAKFAST WITH THE BOWL'S LID USED AS AN EGGCUP. THE SERVICE INVITES EXPERIMENTATION.

The Fantasy

MOVES ON. THE NOBEL DINNER SERVICE GROWS
AND NEW PIECES ARE ADDED.

1994

Nelson Mandela became the president of South Africa. The hottest subject this year was global communication technology. Possibilities were opening up and things that only a short while ago were virtually regarded as science fiction, were within man's grasp. Borders and barriers were being broken down, and the year's buzz words were "internet" and "world wide web".

The Nobel Prize for Physics was shared by the veterans *Bertram N. Brockhouse*, from Canada, and *Clifford G. Shull*, of the USA, who discovered the practical technique of neutron scattering to analyse atomic structures and movement in various materials. The Hungarian-born American, *George A. Olah*, received the Nobel Prize for Chemistry for having harnessed extremely volatile intermediates called carbocations, positively charged hydrocarbons, which turned out to have many uses for the chemical industry.

The Nobel Prize for Medicine went to *Alfred G. Gilman* and *Martin Rodbell*, both Americans, who outlined the G-proteins' significance to cellular communication. The Japanese poet, *Kenzaburo Oe*, received the Nobel Prize for Literature.

The Nobel Peace Prize was shared by *Yassir Arafat*, *Shimon Peres* and *Yitzak Rabin*. One of the members of the Norwegian Nobel Committee resigned in protest.

John C. Harsanyi and *John F. Nash*, of the USA, as well as *Reinhard Selten*, from Germany, received the Nobel Prize for Economics for their game theory.

THE NOBEL LITERATURE LAUREATE 1994,
KENZABURO OE, PROVES A POPULAR CHOICE.

1994 FRESH BREEZES AND FRESH FRUITS. A KALEIDOSCOPE
OF IMPRESSIONS. IMAGINATION IS THE ONLY LIMITATION.

Rolled Duck Breasts on a Salad Bed

Serves 6

350 g (3/4 lb) smoked duck breast
350 g (3/4 lb) fresh chard or
fresh spinach
2 ripe mangos

Salad:
150 g (5 oz) assorted lettuces
2 tbsp raspberry vinegar
75 ml (5 tbsp) walnut oil
salt, pepper
12 walnuts for garnish

Method:

Freeze the duck breast for 2 hours. Cut thin slices, trying to cut them as large and thin as possible. Lay the overlapping slices onto clingfilm.

Bring the water to the boil. Cut away the thickest stalks on the chard. Blanch the leaves for a few seconds. Cool rapidly in cold water. Dry the leaves until they are quite dry. Peel and thinly slice the mangos.

Spread the mango slices onto the meat slices. Lay the chard leaves on top. Roll up like a Swiss roll. Roll in clingfilm. To make the rolls really tight and firm, roll them in aluminium foil twisting the ends of the foil like a cracker. Freeze for at least 5–6 hours.

Take out the roll and defrost sufficiently to cut attractive slices about 1/2 cm (1/4 inch) thick.

Wash and drain the salad leaves. Mix together the vinegar, oil, salt and pepper. Toss the salad in the dressing.

Lay the rolls onto a bed of salad, and garnish with the walnuts.

Fillet of Veal with Mushrooms, Spinach and Tomatoes

Serves 6

800 g (1 3/4 lb) fillet of veal
400 g (1 lb) mushrooms, e.g. shiitake,
cep or field mushrooms
2 red onions
a clove of garlic
3 tomatoes
250 g (1/2 lb) spinach leaves
3 tbsp olive oil
salt, pepper

Sauce:
2 shallots or half an onion
50 ml (3 1/2 tbsp) well scrubbed
vegetable cubes;
equal quantities of
carrot, celery and leek
1 tbsp butter
300 ml (1 1/3 cups) red wine
100 ml (7 tbsp) water
4 tbsp concentrated
veal stock (bottled)
a pinch of white pepper
1 tsp dried sage
1/2 tsp brown sugar
1 tsp cornflour or equivalent
thickening agent e.g. Maizena
+ 2 tbsp wine

Method:

Begin with the sauce. Peel and finely chop the onion. Fry it with the vegetable cubes in butter. Add the wine, water, veal stock, white pepper, sage and brown sugar. Bring to the boil. Remove the pan from the heat. Allow to stand and extract the flavour of the herbs until the rest of the dish is ready.

Mix the cornflour or equivalent and the wine together. Stir it into the sauce. Bring to the boil, stirring constantly. Taste.

Cut the mushrooms into pieces. Peel and chop the onion and garlic. Halve the tomatoes, scoop out the seeds and chop into cubes. Remove the thickest stalks from the spinach.

Cut the veal fillet into 6 medallions. Fry or grill for a few minutes on each side. Add salt and pepper.

Heat the oil in a pan. Fry the mushrooms with the garlic. Add the red onion, tomato cubes and spinach. Heat gently.

Arrange the mushroom mixture on warmed plates. Place the meat alongside and pour over the sauce. A good accompaniment to this dish is Potatoes with Ginger. See the recipe on page 83.

Tip: If the sauce is too thick or strong, dilute slightly.

Dessert 1994

Nobel Parfait Ice Cream

Serves 12

1 round basin,
about 2 litres (9 cups) in volume
1 round basin,
about 800 ml (3 1/2 cups) in volume

Vanilla parfait:
2 vanilla pods
6 egg yolks
150 ml (2/3 cup) sugar
500 ml (2 cups) whipping cream

Raspberry sorbet:
150 ml (2/3 cup) sugar
150 ml (2/3 cup) water
zest of half a lemon
300 ml (1 1/3 cups) liquidised
raspberries

Method:

Begin with the parfait. Cut the vanilla pods in half lengthways. Scrape out the seeds into a pan. Add the egg yolks and sugar. Whisk over a bain marie* until it becomes quite thick. Remove the pan from the heat and continue to whisk until the mixture has cooled. Whisk the cream until stiff. Fold into the cold egg mixture.

Pour the mixture into the larger basin. Put the smaller basin inside and press down so that the mixture rises up the sides of the larger basin and so that there will be a hollow area in the middle. Freeze for at least 8 hours.

The sorbet. Bring the water, sugar and lemon zest to the boil. Allow to cool. Remove the lemon zest. Add the liquidised raspberries. Put the mixture into an ice cream maker until it is creamy.

Remove the smaller basin from the parfait. Spoon in the sorbet. Freeze for at least 8 hours.

Shortly before serving dip the basin into hot water so that the parfait is easier to turn out. Cut into nice segments and serve with spun sugar or a good piece of chocolate.

*Bain marie is an arrangement where you heat a large pan full of hot water and place a smaller bowl or pan containing your ingredients inside it. This gives a gentle heat, which never exceeds 100°C (210°F).

Stockholm the 10th of December

The limousines pull up outside Stockholm's Concert Hall and the Nobel laureates climb out. The lighting for the television cameras and photographers' flashes light up the darkness of the December sky.

The Nobel Prizes have been distributed here since 1926; the year that the building was opened. It is built in the classical style and was designed by Ivar Tengbom. Inside the Concert Hall the guests can admire the best that 1920s Swedish art could offer. They see furniture by Carl Malmsten, sculptures by Carl Milles, paintings by Isaac Grünewald, fittings by Simon Gates and textiles by Elsa Gullberg. On the big day itself, the room is bedecked with thousands of flowers.

All the guests take their places in the Great Hall. The laureates' families sit in the front rows. The atmosphere among the 1,800 guests is one of anticipation. The representatives of the institutions which administer the prizes come onto the podium. They represent the Royal Academy of Science, the Nobel committee at the Karolinska Institute and the Swedish Academy. The media irreverently call the podium *Penguin Hill* because of the abundance of evening dress. At precisely 4.30 pm the king and queen enter. An anthem in honour of the king slowly fades away. The laureates process in.

The Nobel Foundation's President gives an introductory speech before

THE KING AND THE LAUREATES MEET ON THE "N" OF THE NOBEL CARPET.

the prizes are handed out. The distribution of the prizes is, like everything else on this day, a well-rehearsed ritual. A representative of the organisations responsible for the allocation of prizes gives a speech. The king is handed each diploma and a case containing the medallion. The laureate and the king meet on the blue Nobel carpet's "N". The king hands over the prize. A fanfare sounds. The laureate bows to the king, the foundation's representatives and the public. Traditionally everything takes place in a certain order: physics, chemistry, medicine, literature and finally the Bank of Sweden's Nobel Memorial Prize for Economics. Between the prize categories, music is played.

Today there can be several laureates on the podium at the same time. According to the Nobel Foundation's statutes, the prize in each category can be awarded to no more than three people. Only the Nobel Peace Prize can be given to organisations rather than individuals.

The medal was the design of Erik Lindberg, son of Adolf Lindberg, the legendary engraver. In 1901, it soon became clear the medals would not be ready in time for the first prize ceremony. The differences of opinion about the designs and the skilful craftsmanship were time-consuming. The designs, different for each of the five prize categories, had to be approved by each of the Nobel Prize awarding organisations. The Nobel Foundation and Lindberg decided together that each laureate would receive a gilded bronze copy, which would later be exchanged for the real 23-carat gold medal. The medals were completed in the autumn of 1902 and look the same today as they did then.

The Nobel Peace Prize is given out in Oslo by the President of the Norwegian Nobel Committee. Even here the prize is surrounded by royal glamour as the Norwegian king and queen are always present at this event. The medal is designed by the famous Norwegian sculptor, Gustav Vigeland.

All the certificates are unique and personalised. Gunnar Brusewitz, the artist who designed the literature diplomas for more than 25 years, has said that he used to read each laureate's work and was inspired by their distinctive characters. He has produced the certificates for winners including Nelly Sachs, Alexander Solzhenitsyn, Samuel Beckett and Isaac Bashevis Singer. The certificates are handwritten by distinguished calligraphers. As well as the laureate's name, the reason for their receiving the prize is written on the certificate. The artists only have a few weeks between the announcement of the winners in October and the actual ceremony to complete the work.

When all the prizes have been handed out in the Concert Hall, the guests at the banquet make their way to Stockholm's City Hall. The City Hall was opened in 1923 and eleven years later the Nobel Banquet moved there from the Grand Hôtel. To begin with, dinner was served in the Golden Hall, but in the early 70s the event had outgrown itself yet again. So everything moved one floor down to the Blue Hall, which can accommodate 1268 guests. Today the City Hall is a well-known symbol for Stockholm and Sweden. Nowadays television viewers throughout the world have swelled the numbers of people who can take part.

The guests find their places in the Blue Hall with the help of a seating plan. They introduce themselves to their fellow guests at the same table

THE FRONT OF ERIK LINDBERG'S MEDALLION, WHICH IS HANDED OUT AT THE CEREMONY IN STOCKHOLM...

...AND GUSTAV VIGELAND'S MEDALLION FOR THE NOBEL PEACE PRIZE WHICH IS HANDED OUT IN OSLO.

SVENSKA AKADEMIEN
har vid sitt sammanträde
den 18 oktober 1979
i överensstämmelse med föreskrifterna
i det av

Alfred Nobel
den 27 november 1895 upprättade
testamente beslutat att tilldela

ODYSSEUS ELYTIS
1979 års Nobelpris i litteratur

För hans poesi
som mot bakgrund av grekisk tradition
med sinnlig styrka och intellektuell klarsyn
levandegör en modern människas kamp
för frihet och skapande

Stockholm den 10 december 1979

GUNNAR BRUSEWITZ HAS PRODUCED THE CERTIFICATES FOR THE LITERATURE LAUREATES FOR MORE THAN 25 YEARS.

QUEEN SILVIA OF SWEDEN.

and look around in anticipation. To take part in a Nobel Banquet is, to say the least, prestigious.

The laureates and their families are the guests of honour together with the king, queen and other members of the Swedish royal family. Also on the guest list are representatives of the government and parliament, and members of the awarding organisations, as well as leading Swedish and international representatives of science and culture. 250 students also take part, symbolising tomorrow's Nobel laureates.

The orchestra plays the entrance march and there is a lull in the conversation. All rise when the king, queen and laureates slowly descend the renaissance-inspired staircase at precisely 7 pm. It is a magnificent sight that greets the laureates. They have now reached the climax of a dizzy and intensive Nobel week. They have taken part in press conferences and given interviews. They have given lectures on their respective subjects, been the guests of university institutions and visited various tourist attractions. Each activity has been selected with the greatest care and each laureate has received his or her own personal itinerary and programme.

The guests of honour are escorted to their places at the top table by students. The President of the Nobel Foundation's board toasts His Majesty the King. The king rises and proposes a toast to the memory of Alfred Nobel. The party can begin. The food and drink is carried in, Swedish world renowned entertainers perform their acts and the Nobel laureates make speeches. The noise level rises and the atmosphere becomes more and more jolly. The meal ends with the scintillating three minute parade as the

THE STORY OF WHY A PLACE WHICH, FOR THE MOST PART,
IS MADE UP OF RED BRICKS, IS CALLED THE BLUE HALL,
HAS BEEN TOLD IN COUNTLESS DIFFERENT LANGUAGES.

WHEN THE CITY HALL'S ARCHITECT, RAGNAR ÖSTBERG,
SAW THE BEAUTIFUL BRICK WALL, HE WAS SO OVER-
WHELMED THAT HE COULD NOT BRING HIMSELF TO COVER
IT WITH BLUE PLASTER.

AS THE GUESTS APPROACH, THE CITY HALL GREETS THEM WITH CHIMING BELLS, CRESSETS, BRAZIERS ON THE QUAYSIDE AND SEA SCOUTS WITH TORCHES.

traditional Nobel ice cream is borne into the Blue Hall, where the lights have been dimmed.

After three hours, the king and the other guests rise to process out of the Blue Hall. The king and queen take the Nobel laureates to the Prince's Gallery whilst the other guests head towards the Golden Hall and the evening's dancing. When the celebration is over, some of the guests go on to the students' post-celebration party. Many Nobel laureates only get a few hours sleep on this unforgettable day.

To crown the whole event, the laureates and other celebrities are invited by the royal couple to dine with them the following day at the palace in Stockholm.

Thus ends an intensive week. Alfred Nobel can be proud of what he has achieved with his fortune, both for Sweden and for the world.

The Original Menus

Studying the menus from the Nobel Banquets is like reading an historical culinary account of the century. Here we find the 70s calorie packed fillet of beef Charlemagne, the mimosa salad of the 50s and the obvious first course at a celebratory dinner during the first three decades, a tasty consommé.

The first Nobel Banquet offered a magnificent supper with poached brill, fillet of beef Imperial and roast hazel grouse breasts.

The next few years were equally extravagant, for example in 1913 a seven course dinner was served including the classic turtle soup of the time, the now famous Walewska, but with turbot instead of sole, and even artichokes. Artichokes were often found in many of the earlier menus.

The extravagance flourished until World War II, but after the war there was a dramatic change. The number of courses was reduced to three, and truffles, lobsters and artichokes were conspicuous by their absence. At the 1947 Nobel Banquet there were sandwiches for the first course, chicken with root vegetables as the main course and an apple tart instead of the classic ice cream for dessert.

The ice cream bombe à la City Hall was served for the first time in 1945. It is now a symbol of the Nobel Banquet itself and has been part of the tradition since 1976.

In the 1950s truffles and artichokes made a comeback in the menus. But the three courses were enough. For several years guests enjoyed a cold dish for the main course. Cold jellied turkey with mimosa salad was the highlight of the 1956 menu.

Various fowl were prevalent in the 60s as the main course. Then guests were tempted with char from Lake Vättern, braised in dill and cream, and finally, for the first time in 1982, fish was served as the main course. Otherwise meat dishes were mainly served during the 80s. Long descriptive texts first appeared in the 90s menus. The variety was enormous. Pompom mushrooms and pastry made from Jerusalem artichokes with smoked salmon and lobster as a first course. For four years in a row fillet of some sort was served, including lamb, reindeer, veal and red deer. In recent years both guinea fowl and pigeon breast have been eaten.

MENU 1901

HORS D'ŒUVRE
Hors d'œuvre

SUPRÉME DE BARBUE A LA NORMANDE
Poached fillet of brill with white wine sauce,
mushroom, truffle and crayfish tails

FILET DE BŒUF A L'IMPÉRIALE
Fillet of beef Imperial

GELINOTTES RÔTIES, SALADE D'ESTRÉE
Breast of hazel-grouse with
Madeira sauce and Salade d'Estrée

SUCCÉS GRAND HÔTEL, PÂTISSERIE
Nobel ice cream parfait, Fruit Gâteau

WINE 1901

NIERSTEINER 1897

CHÂTEAU ABBÉ GORSE 1881

CHAMPAGNE CRÉME DE BOUZY
DOUX ET EXTRA DRY

XEREZ

MENU 1913

TORTUE CLAIRE
Clear Turtle Soup

SUPRÊME DE TURBOTIN WALEWSKA
Turbot Walewska Suprême

POULARDE MASSENET
Poularde a'la Massenet

CHAUFROIX DE CAILLES LUCULLUS SALADE
Chauffroix Quail Salad a'la Lucullus

SALADE
Salad

FONDS D'ARTICHAUTS MAINTENON
Artichoke Bases a'la Maintenon

PARFAIT PRALINÉ
Praline Parfait

FRIANDISES
Sweetmeats

FRUITS
Fruit

WINE 1913

MADÉRE OLD

1905 CHÂTEAU SMITH HAUT LAFITE

1908 RÜDESHEIMER

CHARLES HEIDSIECK, DEMI-SEC

1904 CHARLES HEIDSIECK, BRUT

PORTO, VERY SUPERIOR OLD

Original Menu 1901

Filet de bœuf a l'Impériale

Filet de bœuf à l'Impériale is a classic dish, which has disappeared from most menus. According to cookery books from the turn of the century, a whole fillet of beef should be served with slices of goose liver and whole mushrooms, as well as veal quenelles in bouquets. Add to that a velouté sauce, a light basic sauce, in this case made from a delicate veal stock, prepared with a light butter and flour roux to bind it together when cooking.

Veal quenelles need a little more work if made at home, but they are definitely worth the trouble. Alternatively increase the quantity of goose liver, or pâté de fois gras.

Quenelles method: Mince 200 g (1/2 lb) fillet of veal a few times through the mincing machine's finest setting. Alternatively ask the butcher to do this for you. Make sure that the meat and all other ingredients are well chilled. Mix with two egg yolks. Then add 100 ml (1/2 cup) whipping cream, a little at a time. Season with 1 tsp salt and a pinch of white pepper. Shape into a bobbin shape a tablespoonful at a time and simmer in veal stock for about 10 minutes. Alternatively grease and fill small round individual baking tins with the mixture. Tap the tins against the work surface. Cook for 20–25 minutes in the centre of the oven, at 120°C (250°F). Test with a skewer to check if the meat is cooked through. Remove and allow to cool a little before removing from the baking tins.

Suprême de Turbotin Walewska

The Polish Countess Maria Walewska (1789–1817), who had a son (Alexander Walewski) by Napoleon I, gave her name to the classic dish Sole Walewska. It is a fish dish made with sole, mornay sauce, lobster and truffles. Delicate, excellent quality turbot (suprême) was the choice in 1913, and turbot, like sole, is a white flat fish with good firm meat. Mornay sauce is a cheese and white wine sauce, which lends itself well to baking in a gratin dish.

Method for a classic Walewska: Poach 6 fillets of sole weighing around 200 g (7 oz). Make a mornay sauce by first making a basic white sauce (béchamel), then add egg yolks, cream and grated cheese. Then prepare some good creamed potatoes (pommes Duchesse): Peel and boil 1 1/4 kg (2 1/2 lb) potatoes. Mash them and add 4 egg yolks and 50 ml (3 1/2 tbsp) cooking oil. Add salt and pepper to taste. Pipe the potatoes around the edge of a serving dish. Grill until the potatoes start to colour slightly. Put the poached fish fillets in the middle. Pour over the cheese sauce. Bake at 275°C (530°F) until golden brown (either in the oven or under the grill). Remove and garnish with hot lobster claws and truffle slices.

Original Menu 1926

Selle d'agneau aux légumes

The cut of lamb which runs along the backbone is usually called the saddle. The meat on the top is usually termed loin, whilst the thin fillets under the back legs are called flanks. Choose a shorter cut of saddle where only a bit of rib is included.

To serve a saddle on a dish gives an extra festive feel to the meal. A saddle with accompaniments such as tomatoes (Portuguese) filled with pilau rice, artichoke hearts and fresh green vegetables was served in 1926 along with a bearnaise sauce, i.e. an egg and butter based sauce seasoned with tarragon, chervil and vinegar.

Method for the saddle of lamb: Trim the outer fat and membrane from the top of a short saddle of lamb weighing around 1,8 kg (4 lb). Mix 100 ml (7 tbsp) olive oil with 2 tsp thyme and 2 tsp rosemary as well as 2 crushed cloves of garlic. Brush the saddle with this and leave overnight. Place a skewer along the backbone (through the marrow along the spinal column). Sear the meat in a very hot pan then roast in the oven for 20 minutes at 110°C (230°F), the meat will be pink at about 70°C (158°F). Allow to rest for 10–15 minutes. Cut the loins off and slice them. Lay the slices back onto the saddle.

Serve with artichokes and fresh Spring vegetables such as sugar snap peas, butter beans, fennel and beetroot. The mustard sauce, see the recipe on page 65, is also a good accompaniment to the saddle. If you prefer a bearnaise sauce, the method is as follows: Mix 2 tbsp finely chopped shallot, 1 tsp chopped fresh tarragon, 2 bay leaves, 10 coarsely ground white pepper corns, 4 tbsp tarragon vinegar with 50 ml (3 1/2 tbsp) white wine. Boil rapidly until reduced to one third of the original volume. Let the vinegar mixture cool somewhat. Put the pan over a larger pan full of hot water and add 5 egg yolks whisking continuously. Then add 400–500 g (1 lb) melted butter and beat it in. Sieve the sauce and season with finely chopped tarragon, chopped chervil and a touch of cayenne pepper. Add salt to taste.

MENU 1926

CONSOMMÉ DES GOURMETS
Game consommé

FILET DE BARBUE MARÉCHAL
Poached fillet of brill with mushroom and tomato

SELLE D'AGNEAU AUX LÉGUMES
Saddle of Lamb with Vegetables

FONDS D'ARTICHAUTS MAINTENON
Artichoke Bases a'la Maintenon

ANANAS À LA BRÉSILIENNE
Pineapple with ice cream, banana and maraschino

PETITS FOURS
Petits fours

FRUITS
Fruit

DESSERT
Dessert

WINE 1926

OLD MADEIRA

1911 CHÂTEAU PAVEIL DE LUZE

1922 LIEBFRAU MILCH

V;VE GEORGE GOULET & CO. EXTRA AMÉRICAIN

IMPERIAL RUBY

MENU 1931

CRÉME CHÂTELAINE
Cream of mushroom soup

FILETS DE SOLE JOINVILLE
Steamed fillet of sole, cognac and shrimp sauce

CANETON BRAISÉ AUX CÉLÉRIS
Braised duck with celery

SOUFFLÉ GLACÉ AU CURAÇAO, PETITS FOURS
Ice cream soufflé with curaçao and petits fours

FRUITS
Fruit

WINE 1931

GOLDEN ORDINARY

1928 NIERSTEINER WEISSENBERG

1924 CH. BEYCHEVILLE

LOUIS RŒDERER GRAND VIN SEC

MENU 1947

SANDWICHES
Sandwiches

POULET FERMIÈRE
Stuffed chicken with celery, bacon and onion

GATEAU DE POMMES S:CE VANILLA
Apple cake with vanilla sauce

WINE 1947

VIN ROUGE

SHERRY

MENU 1954

TRUITE DE RIVIERE FUMEE
EPINARDS A LA CREME
Smoked salomon trout with creamed spinach

FILET DE BOEUF ROTI, FONDS D'ARTICHAUTS
PRINCESSE, CHAMPIGNONS
FRAIS AU PORTO, POMMES PARISIENNE
Roast Beef with artichokes and truffle

POIRES ROBERTA
Pears with pistachio ice cream
and chocolate sauce

WINE 1954

OCKFENER BOCKSTEINER 1952

CHATEAU GRUAUD LAROSE 1950 EN MAGNUM

HEIDSIECK BRUT DRY MONOPOLE

EAU MINERALE DE RAMLÖSA

MENU 1969

AVOCATS FARCIS AU SAUMON
SAUCE GOURMET MOSCOVITE
Salmon stuffed with avocado

FILET DE BOEUF ROTI PERIGOURDINE
Stuffed fillet of beef with truffle sauce

SORBET A L'ORANGE
Orange sorbet

WINE 1969

KRUG, BRUT RESERVE

CHATEAU POTENSAC 1959

MENU 1975

MOUSSE FROIDE DE BARBUE
SAUCE AUX ECREVISSES
Cold timbale of brill with shrimp sauce

POULE DE NEIGE ROTIE SAUCE AU FOIE
GRAS ET TRUFFES GELEE DE SORBES, POMMES
TROIS COURONNES, SALADE DE SAISON
Fried ptarmigan with truffle and goose
liver sauce, rowanberry jelly, Seasonal Salad

PARFAIT GLACE AUX AIRELLES ROUGES,
BISCUITS AUX AMANDES
Lingonberry parfait with almond cakes

WINE 1975

KRUG BRUT PRIVATE CUVEE

CHATEAU LACAUSSADE 1970

MENU 1980

SAUMON FUME AUX EPINARDS OEUF POCHE
Smoked salomon with spinach and poached egg

FILET DE RENNE AUX CHANTERELLES SAUCE
AKVAVIT POMMES LYONNAISE, SALADE ET GELEE
Fillet of reindeer with chanterelles
and Aquavit sauce, potatoes Lyonnaise

PARFAIT GLACE NOBEL, PETITS FOURS
Nobel ice cream parfait

WINE 1980

G.H. MUMM, CORDON ROUGE, BRUT

CHATEAU LANDREAU 1976

EAU MINERALE DE RAMLÖSA

MENU 1994

ROULADE DE POITRINE DE CANARD
FUMEE A LA MANGUE ET A LA BETTE
ACCOMPAGNEE DE MACHE AUX
PIGNONS ET DE SON CROISSANT NOBEL
Roulades of smoked duck breast, mango
and chard maché salad with pine kernels

FILET DE VEAU PARFUME A LA SAUGE ET SES
CHAMPIGNONS POM POM TOMATE FARCIE ET SES
EPINARDS GARNITURE ET CREPES DE POMMES
DE TERRE AU GINGEMBRE
Fillet of veal with sage and PomPom
mushrooms, tomato suffled with spinach,
small potato pancakes with ginger

PARFAIT NOBEL EN VOILE SORBET AUX
FRAMBOISES ET SON PARFAIT VANILLE
Nobel ice cream parfait with spun sugar

WINE 1994

MOËT & CHANDON, 1983
CUVÉE SPÉCIALE 250ÈME ANNIVERSAIRE

CHATEAU LIVERSAN, 1990 HAUT-MÉDOC

MOULIN TOUCHAIS, 1984 CÔTEAUX DU LAYON

EAU MINERALE CARL VON LINNE

GRAND CRÛ
CHATEAU
Mouton Rothschild
1911

Eschenauer & Co
BORDEAUX

MARQUE DEPOSÉE

CHÂTEAU
Rauzan-Gassies
1924
MARGAUX
Mis en Bouteilles
au
Château

Mouton Cadet
Sélection Rothschild
Bordeaux   Médoc

Grand Vin de Médoc
Sélectionné par le Maître de Chais,
des Châteaux Mouton-Rothschild
et Mouton d'Armailhacq.

APPELLATION HAUT-MÉDOC CONTROLÉE

CHATEAU
PAVEIL DE LUZE
Appellation HAUT MÉDOC Contrôlée

A. de Luze & Fils
BORDEAUX

In Sparkling Glasses

At the supper in 1901 the first Nobel laureates were able to enjoy three French wines: a Margaux, Château Abbé Gorse 1881 and Champagne Crème de Bouzy, both Doux and Extra Dry. The dinner, begun with a Niersteiner and ended with a sherry, was very much in keeping with the times and the misspelling of Gorsse in the menu seemed to pass unnoticed.

If the Indian, Rabindranath Tagore, who won the Nobel Prize for Literature in 1913, had won today, the French champagne could have been replaced by the Indian sparkling wine Omar Khayyam, which would have been a doubly poetic homage to the writer.

Even casual wine drinkers would have thought the wine list in 1947 with Vin Rouge and Sherry to be rather sparse. The sandwiches served as the first course would, presumably, not compare favourably either with the buffet of canapés which we have in our menu.

The American prize winners in 1954 certainly enjoyed the German and French inspired wine list to its full. They could hardly have guessed, and nor could the rest of the world, that California was about to wake up and recover from prohibition's hangover. Ten years later the American wine producers were to lead the way in a technological wine revolution which germinated vines and forced wine to new heights of quality in places where previously this could only have been dreamed of. The number of wine-producing countries grew enormously and new areas developed.

Even as late as 1969 the wine list was still completely French. The fact that the Italian, Eugenio Montale, could not be honoured by one single Italian wine in 1975, seems most unimaginative. The next literature laureates in our selection, the Polish-American, Czeslaw Milosz, 1980, and the Japanese, Kenzaburo Oe, 1994, were also able to raise their glasses and enjoy champagne and red bordeaux.

The intention here is not to denigrate French wines, or German ones, or all the port and sherry and madeira which overflows on the Nobel Banquets' wine lists. It is simply indicative of an era, which has now gone. The available range of wines from all over the world has grown enormously during the 20th century and it continues to do so. It is only over the last 20 years that we have opened the door to Australian wine, and less than 10 years since we did the same to wine from Chile and South Africa. It will soon be time to let China in on the act, and maybe even Japan.

Our Recommendations

In recommending drinks to go with our modern Nobel Banquet menus we have limited ourselves to a certain type of wine as a source of inspiration. There is such an abundance of good alternatives offered by today's rich wine world, that the choice can be either quite cheap or much more expensive, and can originate from many different countries and areas. To some extent our recommendations are based upon the original menus, but in order for the wine to better match the strong tastes and challenging ingredients which are used in our menus – horseradish, mustard, spinach, asparagus – we have

gone beyond the traditional boundaries of convention with our choice of drinks and selected wines from all over the world. This is surely entirely in keeping with Alfred Nobel's own thinking.

Our suggestions include wines to accompany the first course,
main course and something for dessert:

1901
1990 Nackenheimer Rothenberg Riesling Spätlese, Rheinhessen
1982 Château Labégorce, Cru Bourgeois, Margaux
Pedro Ximénez or sweet oloroso: Matusalem from Gonzáles Byass, Jerez

1913
1992 Meursault Perrières, Coche-Dury, Côte de Beaune
Light Pinot Noir: Garnet from Saintsbury, Carneros, California
Tawny port, 30 years old

1926
Madeira: Old Sercial or Old Verdelho
1985 Rausan-Ségla, Margaux or Ribera del Duero, Spain: Pesquera, Alión, Hacienda de Monasterio
Sweet muscat wine: Samos Nectar, Greece

1931
Dry Oloroso or Palo Cortado, Jerez
Peter Lehmann Sémillon, Barossa Valley, Australia
Orange Muscat Essensia, Quady, California

1947
Champagne: Dom Ruinart Blanc de Blancs 1988
White rioja: Muga or Sémillon Haute Provence in casks, Franschhoek, South Africa
Pinot Gris Vendange Tardive or Sélection de Grains Nobles, Zind-Humbrecht, Alsace

1954
Grüner Veltliner Smaragd, Wachau, Austria
1995 Lytton Springs Zinfandel, Ridge, California
Tokaji Aszú 4–5 puttonyos, Hungary

1969
Sauvignon Blanc: Buitenverwachting, Constantia, South Africa
Full bodied Shiraz: 1994 Mount Langi Ghiran Shiraz, Victoria, Australia
Muscat de Beaume-de-Venise or liqueur: Créole Schrubb, Martinique; Mandarine Napoléon, Belgium; Cointreau

1975
Cà del Bosco, sparkling wine from Franciacorta, Italy
Rosso di Montalcino, Toscana or a modern barolo from Gomba, Piemonte, Italy
Torcolato, sweet passito from F. Maculan, Veneto, Italy

1980
Dry sparkling wine: Blanc de Blancs Prestige Cuvée from Scharffenberger, Anderson Valley, California
1990 Barón de Oña, Rioja Reserva or Conde de Siruela from Bodegas Santa Eulalia, Ribera del Duero, Spain
Riesling from Jackson Estate, New Zealand

1994
White rioja with cask-like quality or Pinot Gris Vieilles Vignes, Zind-Humbrecht, Alsace
Châteauneuf-du-Pape or Yaldara Grenache Reserve from Whitmore Old Vineyard, Château Yaldara, South Australia
Moulin Touchais 1983, Coteaux du Layon, Loire or Rutherglen Liqueur Muscat from Morris, Victoria, Australia

Coffee

AND LIQUEUR WITH A SMALL BISCUIT PUTS THE SOUL AT EASE,
SO AS TO ENJOY THE BREAK AT THE END OF A GOOD MEAL.

Petits fours

THE CULINARY DECORATION WHICH SHOULD
PLEASE BOTH THE EYE AND THE TASTEBUDS.

Conversion Table

This book uses the metric system because it is the most precise and universally understood. The conversion charts provided below are intended as an approximate reference guide only. A good cook should at all times use his or her discretion.

WEIGHT

Metric	Imperial
50 g	1 3/4 oz
100 g	3 1/2 oz
250 g	9 oz
500 g	1 lb 1 oz
1000 g (1 kg)	2 lb 3 oz

To convert, multiply the number of grams by 0,353 to obtain the number in ounces.

VOLUME

Metric	fl. oz.	US	Imperial
1 ml	0,035	-	-
5 ml	-	1 tsp	1 tsp
15 ml	1/2	1 tbsp	1 tbsp
28 ml	1	2 tbsp	2 tbsp
50 ml	1 3/4	3 1/2 tbsp	3 1/2 tbsp
100 ml	3 1/2	-	-
225 ml	8	1 cup	-
550 ml	20	-	1 pint
1000 ml = 1 litre	35	4 1/2 cups	1 3/4 pints

OVEN TEMPERATURES

Celsius	Fahrenheit	Gas Mark
110°	225°	1/4
120°	250°	1/2
140°	275°	1
150°	300°	2
170°	325°	3
180°	350°	4
190°	375°	5
200°	400°	6
220°	425°	7
230°	450°	8
240°	475°	9

To convert Celsius to Fahrenheit, multiply by 9, divide by 5 and add 32.

Hélène Bodin
ORIGINAL IDEA AND EDITOR

Stefan Bjur
FOOD PREPARATION

Pepe Nilsson
PHOTOGRAPHS

Nicke Ericson
ART DIRECTOR

Christoffer Rasmussen Punsvik
GRAPHIC DESIGNER

Joakim Smith/Tomas Dalström
TEXT

Ragna Herrgård/Sigbrit Kvarning/Janne Rask
TABLE SETTING STYLISTS

Jan Samuelson/Oz Clarke
WINE RECOMMENDATION

Alpha CRC Ltd, Cambridge, England
ENGLISH TRANSLATION

Lars-Göran Andersson/Stadshuskällaren, Eva Bouvin, Ingela Grip, Anders Silvén,
Gunilla Bergh, Anna Kuylenstierna, Willy Ratzinger, Stefan Johnson, Olle Landsell, André Grisell,
Manfred Manhkopf, Peje Hasselqvist, Henrik Ahlén, Boo Jonsson, Nina Alderete.

Thanks are due to: A La Carte Antik, Afrodite antik, Antikt & Modernt, The Nobel Museum Karlskoga,
Duka AB, Gense, Grand Hotel, Gustavsberg Ceranics Center, Hackman Rörstrand, House,
Klässbols Linneväveri, Munka Present AB, Måleri & Inredning AB, NK, The Nobel Library,
Orrefors, The Royal Library in Stockholm, Sia Lustgården AB, Skansen, Solgården Antikt,
Stockholm City Museum, The Swedish National Archive, The National Museum of Science
and Technology, Trädkronan Sundwest AB, Vita Valvet AB, Berntson & Son.

Particular thanks are due to the Nobel Foundation.

Printing   Tien Wah Press, Singapore 2001
Typography   Berthold Baskerville, Trade Gothic
Paper   Nymolla Gloss 150 g

Pictures: April film & photographs/Archive Photos 68, 99, 103, 138, 162. Bertil Strandell 149, 152, 154. Boo Jonsson/Reportagetjänst 11. Claes Löfgren/Pressens Bild 185. Corbis-Bettman 22. FLT/Pica 88. Gunnar Brusewitz/Hans P 201. Hammarsten/IBL 21, 202. Hans T Dahlskog/Pressens Bild 151, 206. Jan Johansson/Björkborns Herrgård 16. Jeppe Wikström/Pressens Bild 204. The Royal Swedish Archives 52. Library of congress/Corbis 33. The Nobel Foundation 4, 15, 43, 44, 45, 48, 50, 51, 55, 56, 201. Ola Torkelsson/Pressens Bild 196. Pressens Bild 58. Ralf Turander 126, 130, 135, 156, 157, 158, 159, 160. Sandels/IBL 194. Stockholm City Museum 12, 18, 106, UPI/Pressens Bild 107, 117.

ISBN 91-973428-2-3

Second edition, first print run 2001